"It is a great pleasure to endorse Barbara File Marangon's book on flamenco and the Ballets Russes in which she explores one of the richest periods in the history of ballet layered with the enduring and evocative art of flamenco. As a disciplined and thorough researcher, Marangon has created a book that will no doubt be of great value as a text, but it is also an intriguing read as it recounts in detail the dynamic intersection of flamenco and ballet in the early part of the last century."

Professor Mary Margaret Holt, *Dean, Weitzenhoffer Family College of Fine Arts, Chair, Regents' Professor, and Nichols Presidential Professor, University of Oklahoma*

Passion and Elegance

This book commences with the history of Indian, Egyptian, Arab, and flamenco dance and then compares and contrasts the history of both classical ballet and flamenco.

The book outlines the early roots of flamenco in India and the journey of the Romani through the Middle East and Europe up to their final destination in Spain. Alongside this, the history of classical ballet is detailed from its beginning in Italy to its later development in France. The book spans the period from the temples of India to Massine's Spanish ballet, *The Three-cornered Hat*, for the Ballets Russes. The chronicle of flamenco's journey from India to Spain is important to understanding the development of classical ballet as it relates to *The Three-cornered Hat*, which is the culmination of the story. The evolution of costumes, space, scenery, and props is examined along with the historical parallels.

This exploration is set to inspire and encourage choreographers to partner other dance forms with ballet as Leonide Massine did with flamenco in *The Three-cornered Hat* while also challenging the anthropological idea of the language of dance movement tracing the migration of people.

Barbara File Marangon taught and choreographed ballets in Italy, the Czech Republic, and Spain. Barbara has a Master of Fine Arts in Dance from the University of Oklahoma where she taught ballet, and she was a recipient of the Ballets Russes Fellowship and a Master of Fine Arts in Creative Writing from the Southern New Hampshire University.

Routledge Advances in Theatre & Performance Studies

This series is our home for cutting-edge, upper-level scholarly studies and edited collections. Considering theatre and performance alongside topics such as religion, politics, gender, race, ecology, and the avant-garde, titles are characterized by dynamic interventions into established subjects and innovative studies on emerging topics.

The Art of Entertainment
Popular Performance in Modern British Art, 1880 to 1940
Jason Price

The Routledge Companion to Performance-Related Concepts in Non-European Languages
Erika Fischer-Lichte, Torsten Jost, Astrid Schenka

The Legacy of Stylistic Theatre in the Creation of a Modern Sinhala Drama in Sri Lanka
Lakshmi D Bulathsinghala

The Canon in Contemporary Theatre
Plays by Shakespeare, Ibsen, and Brecht in Contemporary Directors' Theatre
Lars Harald Maagerø

Passion and Elegance
How Flamenco and Classical Ballet Met at the Ballets Russes
Barbara File Marangon

For more information about this series, please visit: www.routledge.com/Routledge-Advances-in-Theatre–Performance-Studies/book-series/RATPS

Passion and Elegance
How Flamenco and Classical Ballet Met at the Ballets Russes

Barbara File Marangon

LONDON AND NEW YORK

First published 2024
by Routledge
4 Park Square, Milton Park, Abingdon, Oxon OX14 4RN

and by Routledge
605 Third Avenue, New York, NY 10158

Routledge is an imprint of the Taylor & Francis Group, an informa business

© 2024 Barbara File Marangon

The right of Barbara File Marangon to be identified as author of this work has been asserted in accordance with sections 77 and 78 of the Copyright, Designs and Patents Act 1988.

All rights reserved. No part of this book may be reprinted or reproduced or utilised in any form or by any electronic, mechanical, or other means, now known or hereafter invented, including photocopying and recording, or in any information storage or retrieval system, without permission in writing from the publishers.

Trademark notice: Product or corporate names may be trademarks or registered trademarks, and are used only for identification and explanation without intent to infringe.

British Library Cataloguing-in-Publication Data
A catalogue record for this book is available from the British Library

Library of Congress Cataloging-in-Publication Data
Names: File Marangon, Barbara, author.
Title: Passion and elegance : how flamenco and classical ballet met at the ballets russes / Barbara File Marangon.
Description: Abingdon, Oxon ; New York, NY : Routledge, 2024. | Series: Routledge advances in theatre and performance studies | Includes bibliographical references and index.
Identifiers: LCCN 2023057649 (print) | LCCN 2023057650 (ebook) | ISBN 9781032421605 (hardback) | ISBN 9781032433530 (paperback) | ISBN 9781003366928 (ebook)
Subjects: LCSH: Flamenco--History. | Ballet--History. | Dance--Anthropological aspects.
Classification: LCC GV1796.F55 F55 2024 (print) | LCC GV1796.F55 (ebook) | DDC 793.3/19468--dc23/eng/20240206
LC record available at https://lccn.loc.gov/2023057649
LC ebook record available at https://lccn.loc.gov/2023057650

ISBN: 978-1-032-42160-5 (hbk)
ISBN: 978-1-032-43353-0 (pbk)
ISBN: 978-1-003-36692-8 (ebk)

DOI: 10.4324/9781003366928

Typeset in Times New Roman
by KnowledgeWorks Global Ltd.

Dedicated to Mischa Kacharoff

Contents

Glossary	xi
Timeline for Classical Ballet and Flamenco	xviii
Foreword	xx
MARICELLE PEETERS	
Acknowledgements	xxi

1	The Early Roots of Flamenco Dance	1
2	Kathak Origins	5
3	Egyptian Connections	10
4	The Arab Link	14
5	Arrival of Flamenco in Spain	19
6	The Historical Path of Classical Ballet and Flamenco	23
7	Origins of the Ballets Russes	32
8	The Birth of the Ballets Russes	39
9	Leonide Massine and Flamenco in Spain	45
10	Flamenco's Contrasts and Similarities to Other Dance Forms: Character Dance and the Bolero School	51

11	Two Flamenco Dances: The *Fandango* and The *Farruca*	57
12	Analysis of the *Miller's Dance* and *The Three-cornered Hat* Story	63
13	*Duende*	69
14	In the Footsteps of Massine	73
	Bibliography	77
	Index	79

Glossary

Spanish and Flamenco Dance Terminology

Actitud   A sudden, static position. Similar to ballet *attitude* with the working leg bent.
Adelente   Forward, before the audience.
Aficionado   An enthusiast or fan of song, dance, or bullfighting and knowledge of the subject.
Agitanado   Energetic and frenzied style of flamenco dance.
Alegrías   Meaning *alegría*, joy, the flamenco dance most performed.
A Mata Caballo   The last portion of a flamenco dance performed at top speed for applause.
Arrodillarre   To set one's knee down.
Artasi-otsiko   Hitch kick.
Asentado   A stance in flamenco dance with bent knees.
Atras   Behind, in back of.
Aviso   The cue from a flamenco dancer to the guitarist warning of a rhythmic change.
Bailador   Male gypsy dancer.
Bailadora   Female gypsy dancer.
Bailaor   Male flamenco dancer.
Bailaora   Female flamenco dancer.
Bailarín   Male dancer.
Bailarina   Female dancer.
Baile chico   Light, gay, flamenco dances like bulerías, farruca, zambra, and rumba gitana.
Baile del Candil   Flamenco dance by candlelight or gas lamp on patios or inns in 18th-century and 19th-century Andalusia.
Baile de Plaza   Dance performed outdoors in the plaza or square.
Baile Estilizado   Stylized or contemporary flamenco dance.
Baile Grande   A flamenco dance that is serious or profound, for example, soleares and siguiriyas.
Baile Intermedio   Flamenco dance that is neither serious or gay but somewhere in the middle.

Baile-teatral   Dance drama.
Balanceado cruzado   Balanced, swayed in a cross manner from side to side.
Balanceo y Vaiven   The undulating movements of the rib-cage, swaying back and forth, or quivering shoulders, performed by the bailaora.
Bata de cola   Flamenco dress.
Biscas   A swaying movement with knees bent and together as the dancer moves forward on the balls of their feet. Named after the bailadora La Bisca in 1920.
Bolero   Once considered Spain's national dance it was refined by ballet technique and performed with castanets. Often the bailarina danced on pointe in the theater.
Bulerias   The happiest, most frivolous, and improvised of flamenco dances.
Cabriola   Goat leap, slap, or beat of the sole of the shoe in a leap.
Cachucha   The Spanish dance performed by the ballerina Fanny Elssler in the early 19th century.
Caída (paso de)   Fall or drop, mostly used in the *farruca*.
Cambiamentos   A change of feet often used in flamenco dance and other dance forms.
Campanela saltado   Bell shape, circular leg-lifting action in a jump.
Canto Jondo   Deep song.
Carrerilla   Small running steps.
Chinchines   Zills, finger symbols.
Chufla   Light, high-spirited, and happy dance used for the purpose of humor in flamenco.
Cierre   The closing of a section or rhythmic phrase in flamenco dance.
Cigueña   Stork pose in flamenco.
Cimbrado   Bending movements at the waist and torso in flamenco.
Cingaro   Non-gypsy flamenco dancer.
Coletazo   The sudden side movement of a bailaora using the train of her bata de cola.
Compas   Rhythmic cycle, measure of time.
Contoneo   The affected gait or strut of the bailaora.
Contrapaso   A step backward used in all styles of Spanish dance.
Contratiempo   Against time or count.
Convulsion   Convulsive actions of the arms, torso, hands, and face while the bailaora dances.
Corrida   Running steps.
Crotalogia   The art of castanet playing.
Crotalos   Small, high-pitched brass finger cymbals used in old Moorish-influenced *zambras*.
Cuadro   A square formation.
Cuadro Bolero   A square or frame setting for bolero dancers.
Cuadro Flamenco   A square or frame setting for flamenco dancers.

Decalogo The ten basic laws or qualities for the bailaor written by Vicente Escudero.
De lado derecho To his or her right side.
De lado izquierdo To his or her left side.
De Palillos Dances with castanets.
Desplante The flamenco dancer's signal to the guitarist indicating a change, break, or link in the dance.
Duende The "soul" of true Flamenco dance. An emotion coming from the subconscious.
Echado Thrown, flung.
En diagonal anterior derecho Diagonal front right.
En diagonal anterior izquierdo Diagonal front left.
En diagonal posterior derecho Diagonal back right.
En diagonal posterior izquierdo Diagonal back left.
Ensayo al medio Dance practice in the center of the studio.
En sitio In place.
Enterado A person who has complete knowledge of flamenco dance, song, and guitar.
Epileptico Flamenco dancers who perform at top speed and with convulsive movements to please an audience.
Escobilla A brush-like step used to demonstrate the virtuosity of a dancer in a section of a dance. An example is the soleares or alegrías.
Esplante saltado cruzado Setting down the foot sideways in a jump.
Falseta An ornate melodic passage played on the guitar which creates a link in a flamenco dance.
Fandango Means "Go and dance." One of the oldest Spanish dances.
Fandanguillo Small fandango typically performed in the Huelva province.
Farruca A popular flamenco dance that originated as an Asturian folk song.
Filigrana The bailaora's arms, wrists, and fingers, moving like a filigree.
Fruncimientos de Entrecejos The emotional reaction of a bailaora in a performance creating true facial expressions such as frowning or knitting of the brow.
Garrotín A gypsy dance with a rhythm like the *farruca*.
Glisada A slide movement similar to a ballet *glissade*.
Golpe A strike or hit with the foot.
Improvisacion In flamenco dance the artist is free to improvise movements.
Jaleador In cuadro flamenco those that have mastered the flamenco rhythm and accompany the dancers with clapping, shouting, finger snapping, and singing.
Jaleo Rhythmic sound accompanying the performer.
Jota Spanish dance and its music.
Juerga Flamenco get-together or party.
Llamada The bailaora notifies or cues the guitarist of a change in rhythm or section of dance. Also called desplante and aviso.

Matalaraña Means kill the spider. From the *escuela bolera* resembles the ballet *pas de chat*.
Media vuelta semipunta Half-turn on half-pointe. Resembles ballet *demi-détourne*.
Meneo The quivering, trembling, shaking movement of the bailaora while dancing.
Morisca Andaluza The undulating, rippling effect of the torso in flamenco dance.
Mudanza In flamenco, various movements of the feet without sound.
Muñecas Rotation of the wrists and fingers in flamenco.
Olé The Moors of Spain used this expression of approval and it was adapted in flamenco.
Ondulado Undulated and wave-like movements of the bailaora also called the morisca andaluza.
Palmas Rhythmic hand clapping.
Pas de buret natural Simple *bourrée*.
Paseillo A little walk or promenade in a flamenco dance.
Paseo de farruca Walk, promenade, in a *farruca*.
Paseo del Tren Tiny, repeated stamping steps in flamenco imitating the sound of a passing train.
Paso de caderas A step with hip movements.
Paso de Cierre A closing step in flamenco.
Paso lado A step to the side.
Pavana Peacock. A dance performed in the Spanish court.
Pavonear A term used to describe the pompous character of the courtly pavana.
Pellizco Short, spontaneous, gestures, mimicries, or whimsical movements employed by a dancer to heighten the effect of the dance.
Pitos Woodpeckers. Finger snaps.
Punta Tip of the toe.
Quinta Fifth position.
Rastreado Dragging the toe or ball of the foot on the floor, joining the other foot. Also called the "Spanish draw."
Redoble Rhythmic footwork composed of a triplet and single beat in a total of four consecutive sounds.
Remachos Riveting, flattening movements or sounds performed in the *farruca*.
Reposao One of two basic flamenco styles where the bailaora's movements are quiet, reposed, and with plastic poses.
Reverencia Curtsy, bow.
Rodillazo Resbalado Sliding knee step of the bailaor.
Rumba Gitana Gypsy rumba solo.
Saltado Hopped, jumped, like ballet *sauté*.
Salto A hop, jump, leap, or skip.

Seguidillas Joyous dance with a small continuation of steps performed in couples.
Semipunta Half-pointe.
Sevillanas Dances and songs of Seville or Andalusia.
Siguiriyas A dance expressing the sorrows and negative emotional state of the gypsies.
Soleares A gypsy dance about loneliness, solitude, and homesickness.
Tablao A stage where flamenco dance is performed.
Tacon Footwork using the heel of the shoe.
Tango A popular woman's solo. Dance rhythm of South America or African origin.
Tanguillo Little tango.
Taranto In flamenco, the pulsating, steady beat of the old dances like the zambra.
Tauromaquia Dance technique inspired by the art of bullfighting.
Temblar los Hombros Trembling shoulders demonstrating the influence of Eastern dance.
Temblar las Manos Trembling, shaking hands used in old gypsy dances.
Tic A gypsy term for duende.
Tiempo de Farruca Time marked to a *farruca* rhythm.
Tiento The two types of flamenco: one slow and solemn and the other quick and happy.
Torcido Twisting, bending, and turning of the torso in flamenco.
Trencito Quick, staccato sounds on the floor resembling a little train.
Voltereta Rollovers and somersaults, tumbling.
Vuelta A turn or rotation.
Vuelta Cigueña The stork turn in flamenco. One foot pushes from the floor, lifts to the knee, followed with a turn on the standing leg.
Vuelta de Caracol The bata de cola of the bailaora spiraling around her legs as she pivots in one place.
Vuelta de pirueta hacia adelante A pirouette or spinning action toward the front.
Vuelta de pirueta hacia atras A pirouette or spinning action toward the back.
Vuelta de Zambra A slow, rhythmic turn, performed barefoot. It is similar to the paddle turn.
Vuelta en cuartro tiempos A turn in four counts.
Vuelta quebrada A broken turn performed fast or slow with a deep bend in the spine, forward and back, on the turn.
Vuelta quebrada doblada It is similar to the vuelta quebrada but performed with one knee bent and lifted forward as two rapid turns are executed.
Vuelta quebradita A small, broken, fractured turn.
Vuelta volada A flying turn.
Zalema Bow, curtsy (Moorish).

Zambra The most Arabic of flamenco dance performed by a woman.
Zapateado Dance rhythms made with shoes.
Zapatillas Ballet slippers.
Zapato Dance shoe.
Zarandeo Body movement such as swaying of the hips.
Zarandilla Shawl placed on the hips when dancing flamenco.
Zarzuela Spanish musical comedy.

Kathak Terminology

Bharata Name means dancer-actor and also presumed name of the sage/author who wrote the book **Bharatanatyam**.
Bharata Natya Shastra Ancient dance and drama book.
Boles Rhythmic dance syllables.
Celas Special students who were taught the secrets of the art.
Chaal Peacock gait or strut
Chakkar Pirouettes
Desi Dance for pleasure
Gharana The teacher's house or school where kathak students study and live.
Ghungurus Little ankle bells that create music.
Guru vandanan Curtsy, bow.
Hastas Hand gestures that recount ancient texts once taught by teachers who now tell these stories as entertainers.
Kavita A poem in Sanskrit.
Kavita Torah Reciting of the kavita partnered by a dance that is performed with speed.
Margi Sacred dance.
Mudras Hand gestures.
Nataka Word for drama and dance.
Natya One of three distinct parts of dance. The dramatic interpretation of a performer which teaches the audience something.
Natya Shastra In-depth treatise on Hindu drama regarding every detail of dance, music, and acting in a production. A European paragon, a complete study of a play that incorporates opera, ballet, and drama.
Nritta Defines dance—the rhythmic movement of the body—pure dance.
Nritta Hastas Pure dance used with hand gestures.
Nritya Suggests the spirit and character of classic dance.
Shastras Studies and learning achieved by the Aryans written in dance and drama books.
Tatkar Footwork
Tal Rhythmic form of Indian music, similar to compas or counts.
Torah A pure short dance piece to boles, or rhythmic dance syllable.

Trika Pelvic movements.
Tukra Piece or fragment. A series of steps performed at a slow, medium, or high speed in six to seven bars of music.

French Terminology

Arabesque The body is supported on one leg with the other extended back.
Attitude A position of the body supported on one leg with the other raised and bent.
Balancé Balancing, shifting the leg from one to the other.
Ballotté Tossed. Spring into the air, both legs bent, land on one leg, open the other in developpé.
Cambré Arched. Bending the body from the waist to the side or back.
Chaînés Chain. Continuous fast turns in a straight line.
Contretemps Against time. Off-beat.
Détourné A turn in the direction of the back foot finishing with the opposite foot front.
Fouettés Whipped. Consecutive turns in one place with a rond de jambe en l'air relevé.
Glissade A gliding step.
Jeté Thrown. A leap in any direction throwing weight from one foot to the other.
Pas couru Running steps to gain momentum for a jump.
Pas de basque A three count step. A folk dance of the Basques.
Pas de bourrée An old French dance, step of the *bourrée*.
Pas de bourrée en tournant Performed turning, outside *endehors* or inside *endedans*.
Pas de chat Step of the cat. One leg in passé, jump on that leg, so the other leg is in passé, close.
Passé Passed. The foot of the working leg passes the knee of the supporting leg.
Pirouette endedans A turn in the direction of the supporting leg.
Pirouette endehors A turn in the direction of the working leg.
Relevé Relifted. The raising of the body to pointe or demi-pointe.
Rond de jambe A semi-circle with the working leg.
Rond de jambe en l'air sauté A jump with a circle of the working leg in the air.
Sauté Jump.
Soutenu Sustained. The working leg pulls up close to the supporting leg.
Tour en l'air The dancer springs up in fifth position then turns in the air.

Timeline for Classical Ballet and Flamenco

B.C.

6000	A statue found in India confirms the existence of Classical Indian Dance roots dating this far back in history.
2575–2150	Paintings of dance on temple walls in Egypt confirm the existence of dance in the Old Kingdom.
2000	The Aryans, instrumental to the development of Classical Indian, arrived in India.
1500–500	Early kathak dance in India performed in temples parallel to the Greek Theater. Indian temple dancers were brought to Egypt.
600	Buddhism came to Northern India and kathak dance became secular.
540–300	Origins of Classical Ballet in Greece.
326	Alexander the Great arrives in India.
200–300 A.D:	Bharatanatyam is written on Indian dance.
100	(the New Kingdom) A Greek in Memphis, Egypt, documents in writing seeing pirouettes and castanets in a performance, thus confirming the existence of both in this period.
27–476 A.D:	Dancers in Egypt began to form professional companies and introduced dramatic dance (early example of *baile-teatrale*).

A.D.

380	Christianity in Europe—the Church prohibits dance.
400	Romani tribes left India.
530	The Church closes all entertainment venues. Singers, dancers, and musicians must perform in the streets.
744	The Pope banned performers from society, the Church, and Christian burials.
1425	Romani began migration to Spain.
1478–1834	Spanish Inquisition.

1499	Ferdinand V and Isabella I signed the anti-Romani law.
1500	The ghawazee settled in Egypt.
1600	Fabritio Carosa *Nobiltà di Dame*—a book about dance at the Renaissance Court.
1642	Juan de Esquivel Navarro wrote *Treatise on the Art of Dancing*.
1653	Louis the XIV dances the Sun King in the *Ballet of the Night*.
1775–1776	*Travels Through Spain in the Years 1775-1776*, by Henry Swinburne, introduced flamenco to the outside world.
1783	Charles III abolished the anti-Romani law.
1789	The French Revolution and the premiere of *La Fille Mal Gardée*.
1800	The Imperial Ballet of Russia is formed with the Czar's patronage.
1827	Beginning of the Romantic Era of Ballet.
1841	Theophile Gautier wrote about the premiere of the ballet *Giselle*.
1842	*No Name Café* was established as the first café cantante.
1843	Theophile Gautier wrote about Spanish dance in *Travels in Spain* and the premiere of the ballet *La Peri* in Paris.
1862	*Voyage in Spain* by Charles Davillier who wrote about flamenco.
1869	The Golden Age of Flamenco.
1870	The end of the Romantic Era of Ballet.
1906	Prima ballerina Anna Pavlova introduced Russian ballet all over the world.
1909	The Ballets Russes gave its first performance in Paris.
1910	The end of the Golden Age of Flamenco.
1917	Leonide Massine filmed *La Macarrona*.
1919	*The Three-cornered Hat* by Leonide Massine for the Ballets Russes opens in London on July 22 at the Alhambra Theater.

Foreword

Maricelle Peeters[1]

I still remember the exact day Barbara and I met. It was on Friday, June 6, 2003, in Saint Petersburg, the first day of the Vaganova Method Conference/Demonstration. Our shared passion for dance and love for the beauty of classical ballet brought us to this beautiful city. After a week full of inspiration and overwhelming impressions, we went our separate ways again, Barbara in Italy and I in the Netherlands, but we kept in touch. Gradually I discovered that Barbara was very interested in the Ballets Russes period, a subject that I only knew through the dance history lessons I had when I was a student. Barbara piqued my curiosity and I started reading more and more about the Ballets Russes, however still relatively simplistic. But with the arrival of this book, Barbara has completely drawn me into her journey of how flamenco and classical ballet met at the Ballets Russes. Her love, passion, and knowledge are contagious.

This book takes you into the history of dance, to be precise, in the history of *The Three-cornered Hat*, a ballet by Leonide Massine in which passion and elegance come together. I have read this book with attention, interest, and much pleasure. It brought a sparkle in my soul and a smile on my face every time "puzzle pieces" fall together again.

Passion and elegance is like a big box of puzzle pieces to me. As soon as you start reading, sorting the puzzle pieces starts. As you read on, more and more puzzle pieces fit together, until the puzzle is finally complete. Some puzzle pieces quickly fit together. For some it takes a little longer, but what all those puzzle pieces bring about is that your curiosity is continuously aroused. You want to step into a time machine and be there yourself. You discover side paths that are also interesting to explore, the start of another journey. No choreography is the same for me anymore. I have found the taste for more research and background information. A whole new world has opened up for me. From now on when I hear and read about the Ballets Russes, I will always think of Barbara because of her passion, knowledge, and the impulse to yearn for more depth.

Barbara, you have written a truly inspiring book. The true dance artist will certainly appreciate it. I wish your book many readers.

---

[1] Maricelle Peeters is a teacher of classical ballet and character dance/international folk dance. She is author of *Ballet Recipes: The Ingredients of Classical Ballet Technique*.

Acknowledgements

I would like to thank the Massine family for granting permission to view the films of their father, Leonide Massine, at the New York Public Library for the Performing Arts.

A special thanks to Dean Mary Margaret Holt of the Weitzenhoffer Family College of Fine Arts for her mentorship on the project that led to this book. Also, I wish to extend my gratitude to the University of Oklahoma School of Dance for their financial support in my research and to the Ballets Russes Archive for the inspiration to embark on this journey. I want to thank Juana Cala, master teacher and performer of flamenco, for showing me the true spirit of flamenco.

Last but not least, an enormous thank you to my husband Gianni for all his moral support, along with Bepi, Gina, and Nino, who kept me company the long days and nights at the computer.

Figure 1.1 The flamenco dancer Juana Cala demonstrates a performance pose. The form of her hands and arms suggests the connection to Egyptian and Arabic dance.

Source: Photo by Jake Pett.

1 The Early Roots of Flamenco Dance

Serge Diaghilev and his company, the Ballets Russes, have a profound interest for me because of my connection to the dancers—George Balanchine, Alexandra Danilova, Felia Doubrovska, and Pierrre Vladimirov were my teachers. Serge Diaghilev once said, "There are only two schools of dance: classical ballet and flamenco." As a ballet dancer the closest I ever came to Spanish dance was *Don Quixote*, *Paquita*, and the Spanish Dance in the *Nutcracker*. The dancers wore Spanish-styled tutus and performed on pointe with fans as props. In this context, the dancers only imitated Spanish dance from the waist up. Until 2016, I knew practically nothing about flamenco dance, but it conjured up two words in my mind: *passion* and *fire*.

Unlike Classical ballet, which has a vocabulary of steps, a syllabus, and a study taught universally, flamenco has no formal school. It was handed down from generation to generation, and training is based mostly on the choreography and interpretation of the teacher. Flamenco's foundation is kathak dance which has the underpinning of an ancient and highly developed school, the *bharatanatyam*—preceding classical ballet by centuries. But the soul of flamenco is reflected in the suffering of the persecuted Romani population traveling over centuries and continents. So perhaps Diaghilev meant the *bharatanatyam* when he referred to the school of flamenco. Or maybe he suggested the school of life experience and suffering which the Romani population sustained along the way from India. One thing is clear—the two dance forms, flamenco and classical ballet, met and married in Spain in 1917–1918 with the Ballets Russes.

Even before that union, flamenco had evolved starting with the migration of the Romani from their origins in India. It was influenced by Middle Eastern dance along the way, and arrived in Spain around 1425, when the Arabs occupied Spain. In order to understand the acculturation of these dance forms, it is necessary to explore their history. The breadth of the history of flamenco spans the period of the first temple dancers of India in 400 B.C. to Massine's Spanish ballet, *The Three-cornered Hat*, for the Ballets Russes in 1919.

Flamenco's history is divided into two parts. The first part refers to the journey of the Romani from India to Spain with its ethnic and cultural

DOI: 10.4324/9781003366928-1

absorption along the way. The second part relates to how modernism influenced flamenco, taking it from the caves of Andalusia to an art form on the international stage. Both parts together outline the evolution of flamenco from India to the Spanish shores, paving the way to the later connection between flamenco, classical ballet, and the Ballets Russes.

The seed of flamenco goes as far back as India and an Indian dance named kathak. Classical kathak dance began as a religious art form performed in the Indian temples around 400 B.C. and later in durbars, or royal courts, in medieval India. Dance movements accompanied stories and were performed with song and music, but the religious aspect of kathak dance was eliminated in the durbars. During the migration of the Romani, kathak mixed with other dance forms and underwent a slow transformation, which eventually evolved into flamenco in Spain. A modified form of kathak was introduced by the Romani by the time they arrived in Spain. Many kathak dance movements remain the same or similar today, and this gives us a clue to its history and its eventual relationship to flamenco.

Performer and lecturer Wendy Buonaventura explored the early history of Middle Eastern dance. Her research found: "Gypsies of all lands share a common origin in India and a common language, Romany, which is based on the Hindu."[1] The ancient Hindu liturgical language, Sanskrit, demonstrates another Romani link to India besides kathak dance. Many theories, myths, and legends have recounted the migration of the Romani from India to Spain over centuries, and we will explore some of them.

An undated antique documentation exists relating to entertainers employed by the Imperial Court in Kathaka. Kathak dance originated with the Kathakas, or storytellers, and these nomadic minstrels traveled and performed before their permanent employment in the Court. According to very old documentation, it was discovered that performers were robbing the Treasury and they were banished. The minstrels became wandering tribes after this event. However, examinations of history tell us the main reason for their exodus is attributed to the invasion of foreign armies. The Romani did not want to become enslaved by invaders.

In India, the Romani were called Banjara and they migrated to other countries for the above reasons. They carried their arts and traditions with them, including some of the kathak dance form.[2] There are theories that the Romani tribes traveled through Pakistan, Afghanistan, and as far as Persia, the Persian Gulf, and the Arabian Gulf. For hundreds of years, they had earned a living as performers. It is written in the 11th century Book of Kings, "The Persian poet Firdausi brought nearly 1,000 gypsies to Persia to entertain his subjects, but they preferred a wandering life."[3] In all of the countries they passed through, the Romani left behind some of their traditions in dance and music and assimilated others.

From Persia, it is suggested that the tribes split and spread to other countries. Some made the journey into Turkey, Eastern Europe, and Hungary.

The Early Roots of Flamenco Dance   3

The Romani in Hungary were called Czingany and in Russia, Tsingane. From Russia and Eastern Europe, it is believed that they made their way to Spain. Inconclusive theories speculate that other tribes traveled into Egypt and Africa. The professor of Hispanic language and literature, Lou Charnon-Deutsch, extensively researched the Romani in Spain for her book, *The Spanish Gypsy, The History of a Spanish Obsession*. She wrote that the renowned Hispanist *Baron* Jean Charles Davillier, in the 1860s, had a theory:

> Northern Spanish Gypsies were descendants of the Tchinganes, chased from the banks of the Indus River by the invasion of the Tamerlane in the early 15th century, while the Andalusian Gypsies were of Arab origin.[4]

In Andalusia, Spain, the Romani were called *gitanos*. The name means coming from Egypt, but there is no solid evidence that a Romani tribe was there. One theory is the name *gitanos* comes from the Sanskrit word *gita*, a song from India, which is the birthplace of the Romani. However, we can see the similarities between Egyptian dance postures and flamenco stances on the walls of Egyptian temples.

In 1955, Rafael Lafuente, a musicologist who was interested in anthropology, claimed a theory based on linguistic studies and a legend. According to the story, the last Egyptian pharaoh, Psamtik III, was defeated by Cambyses II of Persia in 525 B.C. Cambyses permitted Psamtik to choose 6,000 of his people to follow him into exile—first in Mesopotamia, then into Pakistan, and later into northern India. There they were met with oppression, forced to speak the language of the Aryans, and embrace the Aryan customs, but they made a pact not to intermarry.[5]

In contrast, linguistic research disputes the North African route. Dancer and ethnologist Miriam Philips wrote about this in her chapter, *Hopeful Futures and Nostalgic Pasts, Explorations into Kathak and Flamenco Dance Collaborations*, as part of the book *Flamenco on the Global Stage, Historical, Critical, and Theoretical Perspectives*. She states that "Many dance forms are passed down through oral tradition and kinesthetic transmission, it can be challenging to pinpoint concrete influences and historical facts."[6] An alternative possibility is that they picked up new dance styles while in places located on the caravan routes where a continuous cultural and trade exchange took place. Myth or legend, many *Gitanos* insist that they came from Egypt.

The kathak dance form often mixed with indigenous dance forms during migration. There is a commonality in Romani dances which also belongs to other dance forms from countries including India, Egypt, Morocco, and Spain such as rhythmic hand clapping and stomping feet. Most importantly, the Romani origins in India had a profound influence on flamenco music. Bernard Leblon, professor of Hispanic studies and expert on European Gypsy History, studied this subject. In his book, *Gypsies and Flamenco: The Emergence of the Art of Flamenco in Andalusia,* he wrote:

> Northwest India, the Romani place of origin, appears to have played an important role in the development of Oriental music.[7]

The composer Manuel de Falla stated that the principle ingredients of flamenco's *canto jondo*, or deep song, demonstrate similarities to songs from India and of Oriental populations. The *compas* is the basic flamenco rhythm. It is similar to the *tal,* which means clap, rhythm, or measure in the rhythmic cycle of Indian classical music. Interestingly, the Indian Ragas have a twelve-beat rhythm and sequences that are comparable to flamenco.

The story of flamenco begins with the history of kathak dance, the early roots of flamenco. We are able to confirm information, thanks to the written resource, the *Natya Shastra,* the oldest book on Indian performing arts. But if flamenco was influenced in some way by early Egyptian dance, it is difficult to demonstrate. Egyptian history is less reliable because Egyptologists have uncovered very little written on the subject. Drawings on the walls of Egyptian temples suggest that perhaps some form of dance existed in the Old Kingdom. But we can only make assumptions without concrete evidence.

We know Arab dance influenced flamenco because of the cultural exchange between the Romani and the Moors. Both groups occupied Spain together from 1425 to 1492. In fact, the *Houara* in Morocco execute a dance to this day which bears a close resemblance to flamenco. One thing is certain: the Romani absorbed local traditions, native music, folk dance, and took ownership, on the long journey they traveled before their arrival in Spain.

Notes

1 Wendy Buonaventura, *Serpent of the Nile: Women and Dance in the Arab World* (Northampton, MA: Interlink Books, 2010), 40.
2 Ibid., 40.
3 Ibid., 41.
4 Lou Charnon-Deutsch, *The Spanish Gypsy, The History of a European Obsession* (University Park: The Pennsylvania University Press, 2004), 79.
5 Ibid., 213–14.
6 Miriam Philips, "Hopeful Futures and Nostalgic Past," in *Flamenco on the Global Stage, Historical, Critical, and Theoretical Perspectives*, eds. K. Meira Goldberg, Ninotchka Devorah Bennahum, and Michelle Heffner Hayes (Jefferson, NC: McFarland & Company, 2015), 47.
7 Bernard Leblon, *Gypsies and Flamenco* (England: University of Hertfordshire Press, 1994), 1.

2 Kathak Origins

As aforementioned, flamenco's origins are in kathak dance. The resemblance between the rigid schooling of kathak dance and the spontaneity of flamenco is difficult to fathom, but it helps us to understand the breadth of transformation. There are contrasts and similarities between kathak and flamenco as we know today. The best resource found on kathak dance comes from the writings of Reginald Massey, the well-known writer of Indian culture. His book, *India's Kathak Dance, Past, Present, Future,* concentrates mostly on the origins of kathak up until the departure of the Romani from India.

The history of kathak is fascinating and defines the concepts of the dance form. Classical Indian Dance began as far back as 6000 B.C. It was a part of the ancient civilization of the Mohenjo Daro and Harappa in the Indus valley. A beautiful statue of a dancing girl was found in the Mohenjo Daro area, confirming the existence of dance in that period. However, nothing is known about the steps, movements, and style at that particular time in history. Then around 2000 B.C., the Aryans arrived in India through the Himalayan North-West passages and formed castes in society.[1]

Kathak dance originated in the Vedic period, 1500–500 B.C., parallel to the time frame of the Greek Theater. Kathak groups traveled around the country recounting stories from ancient scriptures through poetry, music, and dance. The word "katha" means story, and "kathaks" mean storytellers. The Vaishnavite Cult had an important impact on the growth of kathak. Followers of the cult worshipped the Hindu god Vishnu. Krishna was the embodiment of the god Vishnu and represented music and dance. The stories of Krishna became a part of the kathak repertoire.[2]

The studies and learning achieved by the Aryans were written in books called *Shastras,* which characterize their cultural heritage. Castes were hereditary and the highest caste was the Brahmin—the intellectuals and guardians of religion. They protected knowledge and shared it only among themselves in mantras that only experts could interpret. The arts had their own caste with experts dedicated to painting, music, and dance, and they formed guilds similar to those of medieval Europe, which were also hereditary.[3] Dance and drama were considered one in India, and the word for drama, *nataka,* is taken from the word for dance.⁴ There was a *Shastra* for dance and drama, the *Bharata Natya Shastra,* which is the manual for kathak dance.

The *Natya Shastra* is an in-depth treatise on Hindu drama regarding every detail of music, dance, and acting in a production. A European paragon would be the complete study of a play that incorporates opera, ballet, and drama. The guide extensively describes gestures, movements of the body, hands, posture, along with costumes, makeup, jewelry, and music tempos for every emotion. The book was written somewhere between the second century B.C. and the third century A.D. The author is presumed to be the sage Bharata, though the name also means dancer-actor. Teachers used the *Natya Shastra* to teach the art of dance, but only members of the caste were allowed to study. However, only certain students, or *chelas* as they were called, were taught the particular secrets of the art.⁵

Sacred dance was referred to as *margi*, and dance for pleasure was categorized as *desi*.⁶ Also, dance is divided into three distinct parts: *natya, nritta,* and *nritya.* The *natya* is the dramatic interpretation of a performance and teaches the audience something rather than offer just pure entertainment. In this way, it resembles the Greek Theater; however, the Greek drama focuses on sound and *bharata* is visual. *Nritya* suggests the spirit and character of classic dance. *Nritta* is the definition of dance—the rhythmic movement of the body. Its clear purpose is pure dance.⁷

In the beginning, dance teachers followed the *Shastras* when they taught their students, so the style was basically the same all over the country. However, when knowledge was passed from teacher to student, it changed a little depending on the region and customs. Dance and its terminology were transformed not only by the region, customs, and traditions but also by the language.

India's early movement and influence in the world resulted from the trade caravans that traveled from China through India and then to Persia, Turkey, and Egypt.⁸ The trade route brought about an exchange of ideas, along with political, social, and religious changes. For example, Buddhism was founded in northeastern India in the sixth century B.C. and began to spread all over Asia via the Silk Road trade route. The arts were not important in Buddhism as they were in Hinduism. So while the Kathaks continued to perform after Buddhism arrived, their art became more secular rather than religious. However, their art continued to be influenced by the Hindu scriptures.

When Alexander the Great came to India in 326 B.C., this delineated another historical change for the arts. India became vulnerable to invaders entering the northern part of the country by the Himalayan Northwest passages. These invaders restyled the social, cultural, and religious landscape of the area. The arts were no longer patronized by religion but sponsored by Kings and Princes. This marked the moment in history when the Kathaks moved their art into the Royal Courts of India. Their large vocabulary of steps, movements, and gestures were adaptable to this change. Religious subjects could be easily transformed into secular. The kathak dancer as a teacher of the scriptures became the kathak dancer as entertainer for the courts.[9]

One fundamental similarity between kathak and flamenco is the "direct and essential interaction with the musicians."[10] Flamenco and kathak are close to the ground which is a complete contrast to the elevated quality of classical ballet. Kathak is "rooted" to the soil and uses similar footwork to flamenco, *tacon,* heel of foot, and *planta,* ball of foot, but it is done barefoot. The dancers wear little bells around their ankles called *ghungurus* that create music. The bells rather than the metal on flamenco shoes produce the sound. Percussion instruments accompany kathak and flamenco footwork.[11]

The dancer/writer Matteo Marcellus Vittucci compiled the most concise resource of Spanish and flamenco dance terminology. The book *The Language of Spanish Dance, A Dictionary and Reference* describes in detail every step. He wrote that the *pellizcos* in flamenco are "short spontaneous gestures, mimicries or whimsical movements employed by a dancer to heighten the effect of a dance."[12] This can also be seen in kathak dance. The *tukra,* which means piece or fragment, is an important part of *nritta.* It is a series of steps performed at a slow, medium, or high speed in six to seven bars of music. A kathak dance pose finalizes the movement and is held for one music bar. A final pose with a bar of music is often demonstrated in flamenco, but in most dance forms, the music ends with the final pose.

Another similar step to flamenco is the *chakkar* or pirouette—an important component of the *tukra.* These pirouettes are executed in one spot at a high speed, and they resemble diverse flamenco *vueltas* performed in one place. For a dancer to learn to remain in one place, the gurus or teachers taught them to turn within a small square of bound bricks or hurt their feet. The peacock gait, or *chaals,*[13] is another similar step and a distant relative to the *pavonear,* which means to strut. The *pavonear* comes from the word *pavon* or peacock and refers to the "pompous character of the *pavana,*" a dance performed in the Spanish courts.[14]

In kathak, *mudras* or *hastas* are hand gestures. The *nritta hastas* are pure dance used with hand gestures in kathak. Along with dance movements, the *hastas* recount ancient texts that were once taught by teachers who now tell these stories as entertainers.[15] In flamenco and other dance forms, the hands work in connection with the arms that express emotion and energy but do not tell stories. Flamenco hands are shaped by the articulation of the fingers which may come from the inherent *mudras* or *hastas* of kathak. The arm movements are circular, along with a rotation of the wrists, and simultaneously the fingers create fan shapes. The entire body produces an image or idea in kathak, whereas flamenco isolates movements of the body.[16]

The school of kathak dance has probably the oldest and strictest training program. Because the dance profession in India was hereditary and based on caste, it helped to preserve the art. The kathak student lived in the *gharana,* house or school, of their teacher. Part of a students' training was to serve the teacher, or guru, and sometimes that meant massaging their feet as a form of humility. A dancer would touch their ear-lobe as a form of respect, whenever the name of their guru was illuminated.[17] The kathak schools were first supported by religion and later by royalty when the dance form moved from the temples to the royal courts. In contrast, flamenco teachers were persecuted by royalty based on the strict laws that were imposed on them.[18]

The kathak dance school teaches the steps of the art slowly, the same way as flamenco and classical ballet schools. When the steps are perfectly mastered by the student, speed is emphasized. *Boles* or rhythmic dance syllables are recited before the *tukra* is danced, and difficult off-beat rhythms are an important part of the early training program. Precision must be accomplished before speed is acquired.[19]

In 1938, the kathak dancer Menaka created a dance school in Khandala, India, and her main interest was using kathak in ballet productions. She produced three ballets using pure kathak dance set to classical music and ballet themes. They are *Vijaya Nritya, Krishna Lila,* and *Menaka Lasyam,* based on Sanskrit stories. Menaka was a friend of the great classical ballerina, Anna Pavlova, who inspired her and helped her with the ballets.[20] This is an example of a later cross-cultural exchange between kathak dance and classical ballet, in choreographic productions. Menaka's predecessor to the cross-cultural exchange of two dance forms was Leonide Massine. The choreographer united flamenco with classical ballet and gave us his production, *The Three-cornered Hat.* There is much truth in the words of Reginald Massey:

> To endeavor to remove all enriching influence in pursuit of some putative "purity" can only result in impoverishment.[21]

Dance becomes richer with the cross-cultural exchange of other dance forms, and flamenco is richer because of its foundation in kathak dance.

Notes

1 Reginald Massey, *India's Kathak Dance, Past, Present, Future* (New Delhi, India: Abhinav Publications, 1999), 1–2.
2 Ibid., 18–19.
3 Ibid., 3.
4 Ibid., 6.
5 Ibid., 7.
6 Ibid., 8.
7 Ibid., 9–10.
8 Ibid., 15.
9 Ibid., 38.
10 K. Meira Goldberg et al., *Flamenco on the Global Stage, Historical, Critical and Theoretical Perspectives* (Jefferson, NC: McFarland & Company, Inc., 2015), 44.
11 Massey, 34–35.
12 Matteo Marcellus Vittucci, *The Language of Spanish Dance, A Dictionary and Reference Manual* (Hightown, NJ: Princeton Book Company, 1990, 2003), 174.

13 Massey, 39.
14 Vittucci, 174.
15 Massey, 39.
16 Ibid., 39.
17 Ibid., 46.
18 Ibid., 48.
19 Ibid., 50.
20 Ibid., 24.
21 Ibid., 129.

3 Egyptian Connections

To understand if there is a connection between Egyptian dance and flamenco, we must first examine what we know about the ancient Egyptians. The book *Ancient Egyptian Dances* by Irene Lexová gives an introduction to the topic of dances performed in ancient Egypt. It is founded on her study of temple images and research articles written by Egyptologists. Based on these studies, it was determined that in the Old Kingdom of Egypt, Egyptian dance consisted of figures and gestures performed in slow or fast movements. Men and women danced together or separately, though more women danced than men because they were usually considered more graceful or elegant. Research also suggested "Men always danced with great spirit, bounding from the ground more in the manner of Europeans than of an Eastern people."[1] The studies exemplify the commonality between many dance forms, including flamenco.

Musical instruments used at the time were the harp, lyre, lute, guitar, pipes, and the tambourine. The guitar is the heart of flamenco pumping life into all its movements and gestures and provides the deepest substantiated connection to Egypt. Time was marked with the feet, which is typical in flamenco. Marking music with the feet was especially popular in solos for both men and women. In addition, the Egyptians used clapping, snapping fingers, and the accompaniment of drums as far back as the Old Kingdom, thousands of years ago.

It is believed that the first time dancers performed the pirouette was in ancient Egypt. Studies of paintings and sketches on the walls of Egyptian temples have suggested this, according to Egyptologists. The *ciguena* (stork) pose in flamenco is where one knee is bent and lifted in front and touches the knee of the standing leg. This typical pose in the *jota* is similar to those found in the temple and tomb paintings in Egypt. The *vuelta ciguena* is a pirouette with one leg bent at the knee, resembling a *pirouette endedan*. The bent leg touches the floor with the ball of the foot after the turn and pushes off the floor to turn again. But we can only hypothesize this pirouette from the limited evidence of a sketch.

DOI: 10.4324/9781003366928-3

A pirouette was witnessed and described in writing at the end of the fourth century B.C., when a Greek from Syracuse who attended a banquet by a rich Egyptian in Memphis wrote:

> These two dancers danced separately or together in harmonious configurations ... while she fled from him constantly, rotating and pirouetting ....[2]

But we do not know what type of pirouette was performed.

While early Egyptian dance may have resembled ballet, we can see some similarities to flamenco as far back as the Old Kingdom. An example of this is the position of the arms. The fifth position of the arms is used in ballet and the *quinta* in Spanish dance is the same. Both arms are over the head, rounded at the elbow, with palms down. Many ancient Egyptian paintings show the arms over the head with the elbows pointed and the palms turned up. This position of the arms is frequently observed in flamenco.

Music and dance in Egypt served as entertainment. Public outdoor dancing was permitted and considered the privilege of the lower classes. While the higher classes could not participate, dancing was important to the Egyptians. For many dancers, there was the desire to excel over others, the spirit of competition that exists for centuries. However, Egyptian dance was performed not just for entertainment but for religious rituals, funerals, weddings, and other celebrations.

The New Kingdom brought some changes in dance such as more symmetrical formations, two women or two men, and groups. More props were used in dancing such as canes for example, which are also used in flamenco. Canes are used to beat the *tiempo* on the floor in flamenco. The following quote found from ancient Egypt would seem to describe a spectacular performance of flamenco:

> The subconscious and undisciplined movement of the dancer turned into conscious and disciplined ones, as soon as the spectators began to be interested in the dance, and accompanied it with clapping hands and rhythmic cries.[3]

Dancers used tambourines or castanets to mark music while they danced. Clappers, or long thick pieces of wood, were thought to be the predecessor of the castanets and are seen in temple paintings from the New Kingdom period. The castanets as we know them today were described in the same letter above by the Greek from Syracuse:

> Then at a given sign, the middle of the hall was taken by a man and a girl dancer who were provided with clappers. These were made out of two small pieces of wood, round and concave, located in the palms, and gave rhythm to the dancing steps when suddenly knocked together.[4]

12 Egyptian Connections

During the first century A.D., dancers formed professional companies in the East and in Egypt. An example of this and the use of castanets by performers can be found in an ancient papyrus which belongs to Cornell University. It is a contract between an Egyptian dancer and her client:

> To Isidora, castanet dancer, from Artemisia of the village of Philadelphia. I request that you, assisted by another castanet dancer, total two, undertake to perform at the festival of my house ....[5]

Examples of castanets from that period can be seen at the Berlin Museum. *Palillos* or castanets are not usual in pure flamenco but used often with *escuelo bolero* or Spanish folk dance. However, castanets are used in two flamenco dances: the *zambra* and the *siguiriyas*. Castanets add music to arm and hand movements, and they produce diverse sounds when produced with different combinations. This destroys the myth that the pattern is always the same and that both hands have an equal function in producing sound. In performances without live music, the castanets shape the sounds compatible with the mood and the dramatic story of the performer. It is believed too that ancient Egypt influenced the frame for flamenco music—both use the Phrygian scale or mode.

Dramatic dance and tableau vivant was introduced in the New Kingdom and was the predecessor to dance-drama or *baile teatral* in Spain. The postures and positions represented in some sketches from the period suggest particular movement dances different from the prior dynasties. The figures are reminiscent of Spanish dancers holding castanets.

Egyptian Dance is different from flamenco because it was said to soothe the mind rather than ignite flaming passion. Dancers were placed in various categories in ancient Egypt; harem, ritual, temple, and vagrant. The harem dancers performed in private for the pleasure of the King and lived within the palace. Ritual dancers were kept in each town for any occasion such as weddings, funerals, and celebrations. An interesting note—the Egyptians brought bayadères, or Hindu temple dancers, from India to Egypt around 1500 B.C. However, the dancers considered nearest to the gods were only the Egyptian women of a high-class origin.

Traveling dancers and musicians are suggested in a papyrus translated from a hieroglyphic transcription of a story pertaining to the birth and origins of the fifth Dynasty kings. The narrative specifically mentions vagrants, who formed groups, but with a permanent base from which they set out on journeys to perform. "They were rewarded for their services with that which was given to them, and with it they returned home again."[6]

Professional dancers living in small villages were called *ghawazee*, and a single dancer was called a *ghaziya*. They were gypsies, as the name *ghawazee* translates, invader or outsider, and were always considered outsiders. A piece of their history is explained here:

> Yousef Maazin, the father of the most famous present-day ghawazee, who live near temples of Luxor, recounts how his tribe originally came from

Persia. He admits that they were cast out of their homeland because (accusations) of their thieving and generally bad reputation and says they encouraged their daughters and sons to become entertainers in order to settle in Egypt.[7]

The *ghawazee* who settled in Egypt came from Northern India or Pakistan. However, they were Sinti, and not Hindu, the Romani tribes who settled in Andalusia. The Romani tribes left India in the fifth century A.D., whereas the *ghawazee* came through the Middle East from India and settled in Egypt around the 16th century. By the time the *ghawazee* arrived in Egypt, the Romani were already in Spain. Again, there are many theories about the connection of flamenco and ancient Egyptian dance.

The origin of the flamenco guitar in Egypt has been proven, and perhaps this is why the *gitanos* believe they have a heartfelt connection to this ancient civilization. What *is* certain—traveling performers exchanged dance movements with other groups when they traveled from country to country, and this contributed to flamenco's exotic beauty.

Notes

1 Irena Lexová, *Ancient Egyptian Dances* (New York: Dover Publications, Inc., 2000), 7.
2 Ibid., 32.
3 Ibid., 21.
4 Ibid., 32.
5 Wendy Buonaventura, *Serpent of the Nile: Women and Dance in the Arab World* (Northampton, MA: Interlink Books, 2010), 47.
6 Lexová, 65.
7 Buonaventura, 40–41.

4 The Arab Link

Around 200 B.C., the Romans conquered Cadiz (Gadez) which was formerly part of a Phoenician colony. At the time, they had the privilege of watching the performances of the famous dancers of Cadiz. Roman writers were inspired by these dancers and documented the introduction of their dance to the European mainland. The poet Martial described seeing the dancers "swing lascivious loins in practiced writhings" or Ovids' description "Graceful her arms, moving in subtle measure; insinuating she sways her hips." The Roman Empire expanded their presence in Egypt, Arabia, North Africa, and Europe from 27 B.C. to 476 A.D., so the migration of middle-eastern dance took place long before the arrival of the Romani in Europe.[1] However, the castanets and tambourines demonstrate the link between the Romani and the ancient Gadez dancers.[2]

Though there are several theories, it is believed that the word flamenco comes from the Arabic *felah mengu* or peasant flight.[3] Flamenco was first introduced as the *Zambra Mora,* or Moorish dance. The *Zambra* is a dance performed by women and in the caves of the Albaicín where the Romani lived. It was performed at weddings and is often referred to as "the forbidden dance" because of its sensuality, and the dance was prohibited by the Spanish Inquisition in the 16th century.

The *Zambra* has more torso and hip isolations than flamenco and "It has a slow, even, marked rhythm with a decided Eastern and sensuous character."[4] The term *Zarandeo* (which means shifting and strutting) refers to the movement of a woman swaying her hips. The weight is placed on one foot and the hip on the same side thrusts out. This is typical of the Romani dances with a Moorish influence. "The *Natya Shastra,* the most authoritative treatise on East Indian dancing, written in Sanskrit between 200 and 2 B.C., mentions similar movements of the pelvis (*trika*) which for the most part have disappeared from India's present-day dance but which may have been taken to Spain by India's migrating Gypsies."[5]

The *Zambra* nevertheless remains the most Arabic of flamenco dance and has many similarities to the Egyptian belly dancing as we know it. The dance is performed barefoot with finger cymbals, *chiechines* or *crotalos, zils* in Arabic, instead of castanets. A *zarandilla*, which is a shawl or scarf, is usually

DOI: 10.4324/9781003366928-4

draped and tied on the woman's hips and used like a second skirt. It is a prop found in oriental dance forms, for example, the belly dancers' veil becomes the flamenco dancers' shawl. A tight skirt with a blouse tied under the bust completes the costume.

Other than props, there are significant similarities in the steps. One example is the *paseo de zambra*, a sideways step used in the *zambra*. The *paseo* is performed by stepping left foot over right foot, then step right on the ball of the foot. The step is repeated several times to the right with an accent on count one. Another step is the *vuelta de zambra*, a typical turn performed in the dance, similar to the Middle Eastern Dervish, the Marwar Nautch dancer of India, and the American paddle turn.[6] The *Zalema*, or bow, curtsy, is the Arab equivalent to the *reverence* in ballet, *reverencia* in Spanish dance, and *guru vandanan* in Indian dance and is executed at the end of the *Zambra*.[7]

In the seventh century, countries under Arab control embraced the Muslim religion which believed the secular and sacred life was the same, so dance was prohibited. However, the Romani were given permission to dance in public places, though the Muslim religion did not permit performing certain Spanish dances.[8] The Koran described the moral way of performing specific dances: "with the women not stirring their feet so that their legs may not be seen."[9] Coincidently, the concentration of work is in the feet in flamenco and the long skirts worn in the dance cover most of the leg.

A dance that resembles flamenco is performed by the Houara tribe of Morocco. The tribe speaks Arabic and is in Inezgane, which is south of Agadir, a few kilometers from the coast of Morocco. Their dancers are mostly men though occasionally talented female soloists perform, and the dance is purely a demonstration of skill. The dance is not performed for religious worship, courtship, or weddings. Observing a Houara performance, I was reminded of flamenco's *bulerias*.

A group forms a circle and sings out loud accompanied by rhythmic hand clapping as in flamenco. A soloist enters the ring, performs rapid footwork along with high jumps, then they quickly retreat back into the group. High jumps are emphasized much more and often in the Houara dance. Flamenco-like barrel turns, the *vuelta quebrada*, emerge in the dance with the *caida* step, falling onto one knee and immediately jumping up from that pose. The *vuelta* turns are performed fast and with quick footwork.

This combination of song and dance is typical of flamenco's *bulerias*, meaning *fiesta*, or *jaleo* from Jerez, the city where the Romani specialize in this performance. The term *jaleo* means sound accompanying performers, but it usually refers to the *cuadro flamenco*. *Bulerias* and *jaleo* invite improvisation. According to definition, the *jaleo* performance can include

> any rhythmic sounds that urge the dancers, who alternate with the singers, such as rhythmic hand clapping (*palmas*), finger snapping (*pitos*), shouts (*gritos*), song (*cante*), and tapping of wooden canes (*baculos*).[10]

16 The Arab Link

Movements from both Egyptian and Arabic dance have been assimilated into flamenco. One example is as follows: the *Morisco Andaluza* is a Moorish movement in the Andalusian style which begins at the lower spine. It gives the torso an undulated and slightly rippling effect as the dancer executes the steps.[11] It is also called *ondulado*, which means undulated and wavelike.[12] Another similarity with Egyptian and Arabic dance forms can be found in the *cimbrado*. It is a bending movement of the waist and torso and gives a lyrical, subtle quality to flamenco and the *escuela bolero* dances.[13]

One movement, the *quebrada,* looks similar to *cambre* in Classical Ballet and is a deep bending action of the middle or lower spine, usually in a complete circle.[14] The most recognizable is the *meneo*, a shaking, quivering, trembling movement similar to the shimmy in Egyptian dance. Also, the *munecas,* the gentle rotation of the wrists and fingers, is a motion that creates the snake-like arms used in both Egyptian dance and flamenco. These movements that belong to the two dance forms are mostly concentrated in the upper torso area.[15] Clearly, Egyptian and Arab dance have contributed to the sexuality of flamenco.

For thousands of years, Europe and the Middle East exchanged ideas, especially in art, music, and dance. The nomadic life of the Romani and other tribes helped the flow of this exchange over the centuries. Once more, there are many theories on the path they took in their migration, beginning in India and ending in Spain. They did not necessarily have to pass through Egypt in order to pick up movements from Egyptian or Arabian dance because random meetings between traveling tribes created this cultural trade.

> The vanishing and shifting of peoples through successive periods of change have left their mark on dance all over the world.[16]

This statement accurately sums up the historical, transformative journey of flamenco through many countries and cultures over centuries.

Notes

1. Wendy Buonaventura, *Serpent of the Nile: Women and Dance in the Arab World* (Northampton, MA: Interlink Books, 2010), 46.
2. Lou Charnon-Deutsch, *The Spanish Gypsy, The History of a European Obsession* (University Park: The Pennsylvania University Press, 2004), 85.
3. Matteo Marcellus Vittucci, *The Language of Spanish Dance, A Dictionary and Reference Manual* (Hightstown, NJ: Princeton Book Company, Publishers, 2003), 87.
4. Ibid., 267.
5. Ibid., 268.
6. Ibid., 255.
7. Ibid., 267.

8 Buonaventura, 53.
9 Ibid., 53.
10 Vittucci, 121.
11 Ibid., 137.
12 Ibid., 140.
13 Ibid., 57.
14 Ibid., 207.
15 Ibid., 138.
16 Buonaventura, 43.

Figure 5.1 The flamenco dancer Juana Cala performing in the traditional bata de cola flamenco dress and costume.

Source: Photo by Okulus Photography.

5 Arrival of Flamenco in Spain

The Romani began migrating to Spain around 1425 as the Moors were ending their occupation in 1492. The Moors who remained in Spain were forced to become Christians or faced expulsion, but they retained their Arab customs and traditions in secret. Moriscos, as they were called, often mixed with the Romani tribes who were also considered outcasts in Spain. This resulted in a cultural and artistic exchange between the two. As mentioned before, an example of this is the *Zambra*, performed by the Romani and attributed to the Moorish dance.

In 1499, Ferdinand V and Isabella I signed an anti-Romani law and many of them fled to hide in the hills. Paradoxically, while the Romani were being persecuted by this law, the Spanish nobles secretly hired them for entertainment. However, the advantage to the Romani isolation for the most part during this period was their music and dance remained pure.

In 1783, Charles III abolished the laws that persecuted the Romani and flamenco became popular outside of Andalusia. Dancers, musicians, and singers began to advance their performance technique because of a new popularity and recognition outside of Spain. They honed in on their skills by performing at *juergas* or flamenco parties, for birthdays and weddings in the late 18th century. Visitors to the region of Andalusia, Spain, described the dancing in street festivals and family gatherings they observed. The writer Henry Swinburne in his book *Travels through Spain in the Years 1775 & 1776* wrote about the dance virtuosity of the Cadiz natives:

> In an instant, as if roused from the slumbers of enchantment by the magic touch of a fairy's wand, everybody started up, and the whole house resounded with the uproar of clapping hands, footing, jumping, and snapping of fingers.

Many theorists believe that flamenco came out of the social and political suffering of the people during the Spanish Inquisition, which began in 1478 and ended in 1834.[1] It was an instrument of expression for their difficulties, and they composed songs that embodied their struggles. In the 19th century, flamenco became an art form, attracting tourists, artists, and writers. They began flocking to Spain, mainly from France and England, looking to experience authentic flamenco dance and music. The visitors relied on local guides for a fee to bring them to performances which were often held in the caves of Sacromonte.

Tourism transformed the dancers, musicians, and singers into professionals and flamenco became an entertainment business patronized by playboys and tourists. Dancers often performed on the patio or in the gardens of taverns and *botillerias* where beverages and ices were served. The *bail del candil*, dance by candlelight, or rather oil lamp, was the type of entertainment sought after in the 18th and 19th centuries.

The French romantic Theophile Gautier wrote about flamenco in 1843 with his *Travels in Spain*. His writings not only promoted the Romantic Era of ballet but also through his travelogue in Spain we have a valuable record of flamenco prior to its Golden Age. Baron Charles Davillier also gave one of the most significant chronicles of flamenco in his *Voyage in Spain* in 1862. The narrative includes engravings by the French artist Gustav Doré that help us to visualize the informality of the flamenco performances at that time—before it moved to the stage.

In the middle of the 19th century, flamenco went from private to public performances. Silvio Franconetti opened the first café cantante, *No Name Café,* in Seville in 1842, and it offered flamenco entertainment on a *tablado*, or floor board stage, and served drinks to a captivated audience. This was a pivotal moment for flamenco because the stage separated the performers from the public and elevated their status and professionalism. In this new standing, the dancers honed in on technique, style, and the creation of new dances.

Cuban music arrived in Andalusia in the 18th century when Havana exchanged trade with Spain. The Romani adopted the Cuban guaracha and created the *rumba gitana*, a hybrid of two cultures and the sexiest dance in flamenco. Popularity increased significantly with the stage venues and the professional flamenco dancer had more opportunities to work. A member of the bourgeois class, who once kept away from flamenco performances, now became *aficionado*—an enthusiast or fan of the art. They began to support it, and flamenco became a catharsis for their mundane socially repressed lives.

In 1917, the Ballets Russes choreographer Leonide Massine filmed Juana Vargas, *La Macarrona*, the famous, popular flamenco dancer. She was called a *gitana* and created a style which has influenced many flamenco dancers. She danced during the period considered the Golden Age of Flamenco, between 1869 and 1910 and beyond that time. With the early 20th century, flamenco moved from the Spanish cafes to the international theater and this brought about another transformation.

Flamenco would assimilate other dance forms in the future with or without success, depending on the eyes of the beholder. It would eventually be mixed with classical Spanish, jazz, modern, and experimental theater to name a few. But it was Leonide Massine's creation of the ballet *Tricorne* that brought flamenco to the international theater beginning with its premiere on the London Alhambra Theater stage on July 22, 1919.

Note

1 Miriam Philips, *Flamenco on the Global Stage, Historical, Critical, and Theoretical Perspective* (Jefferson, NC: McFarland & Company, Inc., 2015), 49.

Figure 6.1 Fanny Elssler (1810–1884) wearing her famous Cachucha costume. This painting demonstrates an example of the early choreographic union of classical ballet with Spanish folk dance.

6 The Historical Path of Classical Ballet and Flamenco

Historical documentations help us to compare and contrast classical ballet with flamenco, including the evolution of costumes, space, scenery, and props. In this chapter, the data is paralleled or interwoven as closely as possible to the time frame of both dance forms. The history of classical ballet can be detailed from its beginning in Italy and its later development in France at the French Court of King Louis XIV. A chronicle is important to understanding the construction of classical ballet as it relates to *The Three-cornered Hat* which is the culmination of this writing.

Classical ballet has origins in Greece that go back to 540–300 B.C. around the same period that kathak dance was recorded in India. Alexander the Great spread the Greek civilization as far as Rome with his conquests. When the Romans reconquered the settlements, they adopted the Greek cultural tradition of dance. The Greeks considered dance to be gestures partnered with song. They gave dance the elegance, style, and beauty, which, centuries later, became the basic form for classical ballet dancers. The Romans looked upon the Greeks as the pallbearers of civilization and admired their art, philosophy, and ideals. Greek dramas became popular in the Roman culture. The theatrical Greek plays included a masked chorus of singers and actors. The voice of an actor was often difficult to hear especially in the immense venues of Roman arenas and amphitheaters. Because of this, gestures became more important than the actor's dialogue and silent acting developed. This was the birth of Roman pantomime, and it would be an important part of narrative ballets, including *The Three-cornered Hat*.

The book *Ballet in Western Culture, A History of Origins and Evolution* by the dancer/scholar Carol Lee is the one of the most informative books on classical ballet history. Lee wrote that when Christianity was established as the official religion around 380 A.D. in Europe, dance was prohibited by the Church and buried for centuries. By 530 A.D., all entertainment venues were closed, and actors, singers, dancers, and mimes could only perform in the streets. They became wandering vagabonds, but they kept their art alive.

In 711A.D., the Moors conquered Spain and brought slave dancers for their own entertainment to the former Christian courts. When they invaded

DOI: 10.4324/9781003366928-6

the peninsula, a fusion of culture inevitably influenced dance in Spain. The Moors encouraged public dancing, especially street dance which their Christian predecessors in Spain had forbidden. Over time, cultural traditions were exchanged in these open venues.

The Pope banned performers in 744 A.D. from society, the Church, and Christian burials. While the Church forbade dance for public entertainment, popular street dancing began to emerge as a physical expression of worship during religious festivals. This form of movement could not be suppressed by the priests and religion. So, medieval dance started as a social/religious activity in public, and with popularity, steps, patterns, and rhythms were created.[1] Steps repeated in public social dances were named and handed down from generation to generation.

While folk dancing in Europe was not the forerunner of classical ballet, it demonstrates the human passion for dance even when it was forbidden by the Church. However, it was the predecessor and underpinning of Court dancing, which is the foundation of classical ballet. In the same time frame, the Romani absorbed local dance movements and steps while migrating toward Spain. Their assimilated movements and steps were also passed down to their disciples.

While public entertainment in Europe was forbidden, medieval guilds kept the performing arts out of the total darkness of religious prohibition. In town center festivals, members performed dances to religious themes relating to their particular guild's patron saint. The guilds competed with each other and created elaborate parades while dancing in beautiful costumes with masques. Eventually musicians formed their own guilds to play music for the upper-class social dances. This position gave them the power to control, supervise, and teach the dances they accompanied with music. So, they became responsible for the music, performance, notation, and choreography of dance at that time.[2]

Troubadours, poets, and songwriters performed at Court from 1100 to 1244 A.D. Minstrels and *joglars* were part of the troubadour's company. The minstrels provided music and the *joglars* performed circus skills such as acrobats, stilt-walkers, and tightrope walkers. Troubadours, minstrels, and *joglars* eventually became one group, and the dancing master was needed to combine the arts in performance. The dance teachers used the peasant dances that developed over the years as the foundation and also refined them for courtly dancing. The troubadours created rigid rules in dance composition and were recognized later in Renaissance court ballets.[3]

In the tenth century, miracle, morality, and mystery plays became popular and were approved by the Church. Slowly dance began to emerge more and more in religious productions. The medieval pageant was the predecessor to court entertainment in the Renaissance and also contributed to the early beginnings of classical ballet. Costumed singers and dancers participated in allegorical themes of medieval life. Pageants incorporated elaborately decorated floats which were the forerunners for theatrical scenery and therefore closely related to classical ballet.[4] At this point in history, the difference between classical ballet and flamenco became very clear. Classical ballet would rely on the development of scenery and theaters to define the narrative accompanying the dance form. Flamenco developed a personal narrative in its painful journey that did not need scenery to give meaning to the steps or movements.

At the end of the middle ages, dance in Europe began to emerge from centuries of darkness. The Renaissance was the rebirth of a new age of enlightenment, and Italy was at the center of this new era. The idea of the Renaissance was based on the ancient Greek concept of the potential of human ability and creativity. The fall of the Byzantine Empire to the Ottoman Turks in 1453 A.D. sent a huge number of scholars and artists to flee to Italy. Their wealth of knowledge launched the idea of humanism. At the same time, rich Italian merchants became patrons to the new migration of scholars and artists. Parallel to the beginning of this period was the arrival of the Romani in Spain, notably in the area of Barcelona from 1447.

The Byzantine influence, which can be traced back to the Greeks and before that to the Egyptians, would eventually spread to Spain. It was significant to the birth of flamenco music. The Gregorian chant, created from Byzantine music, became important in the Spanish Church. It can be felt in the *canto jondo*, certain *seguiriyas*, and in deep-song or tragic themes. The *canto jondo* music developed from the social and political migration of the Muslim invasion and the arrival of the Romani in Spain. From the Orient, the Romani carried the songs of their ancestors and integrated them with local music.[5] East met west and a new style of music was created.

Gradually, the strong hold of the Church on the European population was diminished when the Renaissance was born.[6] Dance became significant with the Renaissance society's new commitment to science and the arts. Spectacular entertainment became less religious and more politically orientated. Singing and dancing were presented during interludes between mythological and allegorical spectacles.[7] At this time, dancing was very important in Italy and Milan became Europe's center for dance. The ideas of the Italian Renaissance quickly spread to France.

By the end of the 15th century, Granada, the last stronghold of the Moors, surrendered. The Spanish Inquisition, which began in 1478 A.D., continued to persecute non-Christian religions. Spanish Muslims were forced to become Christians, and during that same period, the Romani were forced into settlement by law in Spain or risk death. In 1499 A.D., Ferdinand of Aragon and Isabella of Castile established laws against the nomadic lifestyle of the Romani. At the time of persecution, the Romani took refuge in caves, especially in Granada. So in part, the art of flamenco developed into a form of expression born out of the pain suffered by this persecuted population.

Twenty years later, Catherine de Medici was born on April 13, 1519, and she became the leading innovator in shifting dance dominance in Italy to France. Under her reign, the *Ballet de Cour* became solidly planted in French culture. In 1533, Catherine, the daughter of Lorenzo di Medici, the most important patron of Italian Renaissance, became Queen of France by marriage. She brought Italian artists, composers, designers, and dancing masters to the French Court. Her lavish spectaculars that were made for political propaganda are recorded in designs, paintings, and literature. The number of dances and dancers are described in these records along with patterns in various writings, but the steps and choreography, unfortunately, were not preserved.[8]

In the late Renaissance, 1550–1610, an Italian by the name of Fabritio Caroso wrote the *Nobilità di Dame* and began to codify steps, create rules, and document dances. Dance at the Renaissance Court usually took place in a ballroom, and it was considered an essential part of social flirtation, so most of the choreographic composition was created for couples or groups of couples. However, the diligent preparation of the dancers to impress the spectators at the Court gave theatricality to the dances.

Though Caroso's choreography in the *Nobilità di Dame* was created for social dancing in a ballroom and not for theatrical performance on stage, his *Notes on Style* reflected similar rules to classical ballet as we know today. Dancers of the Renaissance projected nobility by their manners, and ballet dancers continue this quality in performance. "Caroso's idea of noble beauty included erect posture, quiet arms, level gaze, and straight legs." He added other important qualities: "Vigor and elegance should combine in a style essentially of strong leg and footwork." These are principles of classical ballet.[9]

Le Ballet Comique de la Reine, or the Dramatic Ballet of the Queen, is considered by dance historians to be the first ballet. It was performed in 1581 and incorporated music, dance, verse, and scenery. The ballet reflected the philosophical, ethical, and political ideas of that period. The production was the creation of Balthasar de Beaujoyeulx, hired by Catherine de Medici as court dancing master. The venue was the salon of the Petit-Bourbon palace in the Louvre, and the performing space was a three-quarters-in-the-round area.

The 9,000–10,000 spectators for the one-time-only spectacle watched from galleries above the dance floor as the entire action was directed to the Royal family sitting at one end of the salon. Free-standing scenery created the atmosphere for the narrative. This was the precursor for theaters and ballet productions as the Renaissance period came to a close in 1600.[10] Free-standing scenery was a significant innovation and gave dimension to stage sets in classical ballet thereafter. An example of this is the Miller's house and the village bridge in *The Three-cornered Hat,* 300 years later.

Le Déliverance De Renaud or The Liberation of Renaud was presented in 1617 in honor of King Louis XIII. It was the next important step in the theatrical art of classical ballet. The performance was held in the *Grand Salle* of the Louvre with a proscenium arch stage and a fixed backdrop with shifting scenery. At the end of the performance, the dancers would descend from the stage and dance with the audience. The 17th century marked the beginning of public theaters. In 1637, Cardinal Richelieu, the minister for King Louis XIV, built the most advanced theater in Paris, Palais Royal.[11]

While classical ballet was emerging in France, the art of flamenco receded into the background by force in Spain. Four years earlier, in 1633, the Law of Philip IV prohibited the Romani from their traditions, especially entertainment.[12] The caves where the Romani hid would be their simple, unembellished theaters. However, Spanish social dancing in the 17th century was not prohibited. In 1642, Juan de Esquivel Navarro wrote the *Treatise on the Art of Dancing* in Seville on this topic. The book demonstrates that this form of dance was accepted by Spanish society.

Dancer and exponent of Spanish court dance Ana Yepes contributed the chapter, *From the Jácara to the Sarabande,* in the book *Flamenco on the Global Stage, Historical, Critical, and Theoretical Perspectives.* She wrote that one of the Spanish court dances, also performed in the theater, was the *Zarabanda,* which has Arab influences. This dance has similar steps, arm movements, and rhythm to flamenco and is considered one of the forerunners to the dance form. Later the *sarabande* became popular in France, surviving as a stage dance and evolving into the classical ballet repertory of steps by the French academy.[13]

By 1645, ballet was confined to the stage area, and the proscenium stage meant a change in choreography. Dancers needed to move from side to side on the elevated stage, so this meant there was a need for more turnout. Vertical dimensions were important now, so steps with elevation became necessary. The performance was no longer for social reasons but theatrical entertainment. One of the most significant changes was the separation of the audience from the dancers. The dancers no longer descended from the stage into the public at the end of the performance. The greatest idea that the Renaissance took from antiquity was to build special places for entertainment, so theaters became the permanent home for theatrical dancing.[14]

French King Louis XIV brought on the baroque period of ballet which united myth and fable to music and dance. Poetry, song, and costumes were elevated to the next level of sophistication along with the machines that created artistic special effects. The baroque period was the response to the strict aesthetics of the Protestant Reformation. For the court ballet, the King built the lavish palace of Versailles in the French countryside.

Louis XIV was a great ballet patron, took dance lessons every day, and appeared in many ballets. In 1653, he is remembered for his role as *Apollo.* This earned him the title of *Sun King* in *Le Ballet de la Nuit* or *The Ballet of the Night*, prepared by Jean-Baptiste Lully.[15] Lully was a dancer and composer of ballet music who worked for King Louis XIV.[16] He also worked with Pierre Beauchamp, noted for his new concepts in ballet composition, and both worked with the French playwright Molière. Beauchamp and Lully believed dancing should relate to dialogue and plot.[17]

In 1713, the Académie Royale de Musique became a training school for dancers under the order and signature of King Louis XIV and the direction of Lully, Beauchamp, and Molière. Theatrical ballets were created through an established program in the early 18th century. Later, in 1784, the first children's school for future dancers was formed within the Académie.[18] The Académie Royale de Danse began to give French names to ballet steps, new and old, many originally from the Renaissance.

In contrast, children studied flamenco with their elders long before the opening of the first ballet academy. The first flamenco academy came much later and was non-academic. It opened in Seville in 1920 and was directed by the dancer "Frasquillo", Francesco León Fernández, 1898–1940, who taught what he danced. Flamenco used Spanish names for their steps, and they continue to use this terminology today.

Professional ballet advanced quickly with the introduction of the *danse d'école*. The Italian art form of comedy, acrobatic dancing, and pantomime, *commedia dell'arte*, which dated back to the 16th century, ultimately changed the strict formality of the French ballet school. Productions that were more geared to country life, based on the Italian characters of *commedia dell'arte*, appealed to the middle class and were very successful. The *commedia dell'arte* was the precursor to the *ballet d'action*, which is action and gesture with dance as the story line. Both the *commedia dell'arte* and the *ballet d'action* eventually succeeded as the foundation and inspiration for the *Tricorne*.

In the 18th century, Charles III in Spain abolished the 1499 law against the Romani which enabled them to come out of hiding. Some of them settled down in *gitanerias,* or gitano quarters, which were often the caves where they had sought refuge from persecution in previous times.[19] The traditions and culture of Andalusia were more compatible with the customs of the Orient than other parts of Spain because it had been the heart of Arab rule. The Romani had already absorbed the customs of the Middle East over their long migration from their genesis in India, so they found Andalusia welcoming. An acculturation had begun between the two groups of people which eventually led to flamenco. As the *gitanos* emerged from hiding, they assimilated the local traditions in music and dance. They performed this cultural hybrid for the audience of the region, taking flamenco to the next level.

While the Spanish monarchy liberated the Romani, and Europe embraced the innovations of choreographers, professional ballerinas contributed to the advancement of the art of classical ballet. La Camargo (1710–1770) performed light, brilliant footwork and excellent jumps, so it was necessary for her to modify her costumes by shortening her skirt and removing the heels from her shoes.[20] In contrast, the long skirts and dresses, *bata de cola*, worn by female flamenco dancers remained more or less the same for centuries.

By 1776, the choreographer Jean Georges Noverre's ideas influenced ballet in most of the capitals of Europe.[21] Noverre's determination to change choreography, productions, costumes, scenery, music, and teaching methods was resisted by those who believed in conservatism and tradition. However, his writings, *The Letters on Dancing and Ballets*, reflected his ideas and the progress he made toward the advancement of classical ballet. One of the principles of his dramatic ballet was the elimination of masques and the use of stage makeup instead. Primary was his idea that "the validity and sincerity of gestural expression"[22] was crucial. Flamenco dancers never used masques because their dancing has always been a form of deeply felt expression.

Jean Dauberval (1742–1806) was influenced by Noverre's theories, and in 1789, he choreographed *La Fille Mal Gardee* or the un-chaperoned daughter. The rustic story is considered to be the oldest classical ballet and a fine example of the *ballet d'action*. The ballet premiered 13 days before the French Revolution. It was dedicated to the common people, like the *Tricorne*, rather than great heroes or wealthy kings, and it also represented the style of the Italian *commedia dell'arte*. Another disciple of Noverre was Salvatore Vigano (1769–1821). He is considered to be "the first choreographer to come close to achieving the ancient ideal of perfect synthesis of music, dance, and mime." His work at that time was named *coreodramma*.[23] This composite of music, dance, and mime was essential to ballets like *The Three-cornered Hat*.

The turn of the century ended an exciting period of development in classical ballet, and the 19th century marked the beginning of the Romantic Era. It was considered the violent response to the political, philosophical, social, and economic sentiments of this time in history. Similarly, flamenco was the rebellious reaction to the historical sufferance of the Romani. The Romantic Era followed the dramatic onset of the French Revolution and the start of the Industrial Revolution, which brought social and economic change in Europe. Romanticism was the philosophy of emotion and individualism in the arts, the opposite of the prior belief in rational ideas.

The Romantic Era continued where the Middle Ages left off and followed the Gothic theme. The ballets of this period had deep emotional content, concentrated around unrequited love stories, and the other worldliness of *Sylphs* and *Willis*. The female dancer became more important than her male counterpart because the protagonist of the narrative was usually the ballerina. At that time, Paris and London became the capitals of the Romantic ballet.[24]

One of the greatest ballets of the Romantic Era was *La Sylphide*, or *The Sylph*, presented for the first time in 1832. Jumping steps were perfected in order to create an ethereal effect and contrast the real from the unreal. Gas lights were introduced in the theater which created bluish, surreal lighting onstage. There were trap doors to make a dancer magically appear or disappear and wiring to fly the dancer high above the stage.

The most important innovation was the pointe shoe introduced by Marie Taglioni, the ballerina who performed the ballet. Taglioni was the "symbol of Romantic ballet's Golden Age," beginning in 1832 and ending around 1870. *La Sylphide* became the first ballet to be danced on *pointe*, and the tradition of *pointe* work is essential today to the classical ballet art form.[25] The same metamorphosis took place with flamenco. It transitioned over time from its barefoot kathak origins to a form of dance with heeled shoes.

The ballet *Giselle* premiered in 1841 and was considered the "creative high point" of the Romantic ballet. The story had origins in Gothic legend, and the ballerina Carlotta Grisi was chosen to dance the lead role. *Giselle* is the culmination and masterpiece of the Romantic Era of ballet. Formal pantomime was not used, but while the choreography was presented for a pure dancing experience, it conveyed the message of the story.[26] At the same time, in 1842, flamenco made its debut on a stage in the *café cantante*.

A well-known ballerina of this period was the Austrian Fanny Elssler, 1810–1884, acclaimed as a dramatic dancer. She had learned the various folk dances of Spain along with the balletic style of the *escuela bolero* of the 18th century. This was the first experimentation with Spanish dance by a classical ballet dancer before Massine introduced flamenco with ballet. In 1836, she choreographed and performed the *Cachucha* at the Paris Opera. She was hailed as the "Spaniard of the North" for her skillful and passionate dancing that made her and the *Cachucha* a legend.[27]

By 1850, classical ballet flourished all over Europe while flamenco dance was developing a repertory in music cafés all over Spain. Flamenco became a singular art in the 18th and 19th centuries.[28] The Golden Age of Flamenco commenced in 1869 as the Golden Age of the Romantic ballet declined. Arthur Saint-Léon's ballet *Coppélia* marked the end of a great era in classical ballet in 1870.

The greatest Flamenco artists began to emerge in the Golden Age of Flamenco. One was the famous *bailadora*, Juana Vargas, who appears in the 1917 film by Massine and who danced beyond the end of the Golden Age of Flamenco in 1910. As the 20th century loomed on the horizon, both dance forms traveled along parallel tracks that would meet in 1918 with Diaghilev's *Ballets Russes*, where they would have a profound effect on each other.

Notes

1. Carol Lee, Ballet in Western Culture, A History of Its Origins and Evolution (Needham Heights, MA: Allyn and Bacon, 1999), 1–8.
2. Ibid., 6–8.
3. Ibid., 16–19.
4. Ibid., 19–20.
5. Bernard Leblon, Gypsies and Flamenco (England: University of Hertfordshire Press, 1994), 5, 72.
6. Lee, 24–25.
7. Ibid., 28.
8. Lee, 24–28.
9. Fabritio Caroso, Nobilità di Dame, 1600, trans. and ed. Julia Sutton (New York: Dover Publications, Inc., 1995), 368.
10. Lee, 44–45.
11. Ibid., 58.

12 Leblon, 21.
13 Ana Yepes, Flamenco on the Global *Stage*, Historical, Critical, and Theoretical Perspectives (Jefferson, NC: McFarland & Company, Inc., 2015), 56–65.
14 Lee, 55–61.
15 Ibid., 65–68.
16 Ibid., 73.
17 Ibid., 75.
18 Ibid., 77.
19 Leblon, 17, 31.
20 Lee, 95–96.
21 Ibid., 108.
22 Ibid., 110–11.
23 Ibid., 116.
24 Ibid., 133–38.
25 Ibid., 140–44.
26 Ibid., 153–55.
27 Matteo Marcellus Vittucci, The Language of Spanish Dance, A Dictionary and Reference Manual. 2nd ed. (Hightstown, NJ: Princeton Book Company Publishers, 2003), 43.
28 Leblon, 56.

7 Origins of the Ballets Russes

The history of Russian ballet is critical to this story, and separate from the history of classical ballet, because it shapes our understanding of Diaghilev's Ballets Russes. Russian folk dancing thrived from as early as the tenth century, and invasions, because of the proximity to foreign lands, helped to develop Russian folk dance over time. While the Romani assimilated the local dances of the country that they traveled through, the Russians absorbed dance forms from the encounter with those who passed through their land. Again, the movement of people for political, social, and economic reasons created new dances or added to old ones.

Around 1250, street entertainers traveled all over Russia and dancers often contributed to these shows. However, in the middle of the 16th century, the Russian Orthodox Church prohibited the street entertainers from continuing their performances. This was around the same period the monarchy in Spain had outlawed the Romani from their nomadic existence, threatening their cultural traditions. Russia and Spain shared a similar timeline of prohibition, while in Europe, the Renaissance was at its peak, and the foundation of classical ballet was being constructed.[1]

The lavish court ballets of Louis XIV received loud acclaim in Russia, as diplomats and travelers would recount the splendor of entertainment in France. The Russian nobility praised the Romanov court when they tried to imitate these spectacles, even though they fell short of the bravura of their French peers. When the Russian Czar Peter the Great toured Europe in 1697, the trip changed the cultural destiny of Russia. After observing western culture, he decided to Europeanize his country by inviting the best artists, architects, engineers, and scientists from Europe to westernize Russia.

Peter the Great restored the capital city of St. Petersburg with Italian palaces and Austrian decoration. The baroque fashion style was adopted and mastering the French language became an objective for the nobility. After Peter the Great traveled across Europe, he acquired a taste for theatrical dancing, especially the masked ballets in Paris, and introduced them in his court.[2] Again, the idea of encounter between Europe and Russia in the 18th century brought an exchange which would later inspire Diaghilev's Ballets Russes.

DOI: 10.4324/9781003366928-7

Dancing masters were necessary to teach enthusiastic nobles social dance. Under Peter's successor, Czarina Anna, the French ballet master Jean Baptiste Landé taught Russian cadets court dances. Later, he asked permission to teach beyond ballroom dance and begin a *danse d'école*. He presented his students in the opera *La Forza dell'amore e dell'odio* in 1736, and this marked the first professional ballet *divertissement* in Russia. Following this debut, the St. Petersburg Ballet School was formed in 1736 and eventually moved to the Imperial Palace.

The first professional ballet dancers, teachers, and choreographers came from France and Italy.[3] An Italian named Fossano took over the dance school after Landé. As a successful pantomime artist from the *Commedia d'arte*, he taught his students acrobatic jumps which enriched the dance form. Later, the *Commedia d'arte* became the underpinning of Leonide Massine's *The Three-cornered Hat* for the Ballets Russes, with satire, dancing, and stereotype roles.

Empress Marie Thérèse of Austria sent her ballet master, Hilverding, to St. Petersburg to raise the quality of ballet in the Russian court, and he presented the *ballet d'action* in Russia. Ballet in Russia did not have to overcome the European structure of opera and dance together and was presumed to be a separate art from the very beginning. The most famous Czarina of all, Catherine the Great, came to power in 1762 and carried dance to the next level. She established Russia as a European power, and in 1766, she instituted the Directorate of the Imperial Theaters which gave tremendous support to the performing arts. During her reign, she built two large theaters in Moscow and St. Petersburg with the capacity to contain large-scale ballet and opera productions.

While Catherine ruled, wealthy landowners formed ballet schools and constructed theaters on their land. Foreign dance masters instructed the landowner's serfs, thus creating serf dancers who are considered to be a phenomenon in Russian culture.[4] A similar comparison can be made to the slave dancers brought to Spain by the Moors in 711 to dance at their court. By 1800, serf dancers were absorbed into the dance companies of the Imperial Theaters because the expense of training these dancers was too much for landowners to sustain.[5]

Hilverding's student, Gasparo Angiolini, became the ballet master for the Imperial Ballet in 1766 and worked for many years in Russia making a great impact on ballet. As a choreographer, Angiolini mounted old and new productions, choosing Russian stories and folklore for themes. The custom of a foreign choreographer mounting ballets based on stories and themes of their adoptive country has been repeated in history. One example is Massine, a Russian choreographer, and his Spanish ballet *The Three-cornered Hat*. Angiolini believed that ballet conveyed its full potential of beauty when it stirred the emotions of its audience.[6] The idea that dance is beautiful when it stirs the emotions of its audience is not unique to classical ballet but is also valid in flamenco dance, which tells the emotional story of its people.

The 18th-century French ballet master, Charles-Louis Didelot, is remembered in dance history as the father of Russian ballet. He made his debut as a choreographer with *Apollo et Daphne* in 1802 at the Hermitage Theater in Russia. As a teacher in the *danse d'école*, he took his students to a high technical level, especially with *pas de deux* work. Didelot taught supported *arabesques* and supported *pirouettes* in classical ballet.[7] In stage production, he is credited with the advancement of flying dancers in a seemingly effortless manner and to the amazement of his audience.

During the War of 1812, Didelot was forced to leave Russia and eventually returned to France where he briefly directed the Paris Opera. When the war was over, he returned to Russia.[8] As a choreographer, he combined the classical enlightenment of Noverre with the emotionalism of the Romantic Era. Danced mime and mimed dance was developed by Didelot and remains a great endowment to the patrimony of classical ballet.[9] Massine later set out to demonstrate this in the *Tricorne* by dancing mime and miming dance, especially in his role of the Miller. While Didelot's accomplishments in pedagogy were outstanding, his goal was to make ballet "the soulful expression of an idea."[10]

St. Petersburg was at its peak in theater, opera, and ballet by the early 19th century. With the patronage of the Czar, the Imperial Ballet of Russia emerged as an important ballet company. The Romantic era of ballet brought many foreign artists to Russia. French and Italian dancers, dancing masters, and choreographers were welcomed in St. Petersburg and Moscow. One of the famous guest artists was Marie Taglioni, and she was followed by other ballerinas of the Romantic Ballet, Elssler, Grisi, and Cerrito. The French choreographer, Jules Perrot, was engaged as the ballet master for the Imperial Ballet in 1849. He revised the choreography for the ballet *Giselle* in Russia and reclaimed his right as co-author. The influence of foreign artists brought the Romantic era to the doorstep of Russia.[11]

Perrot filled the void left by Didelot at the Imperial ballet ten years before. He was praised by the Russian people and named the "poet of movement".[12] Arthur Saint-Léon succeeded Perrot and created the famous ballet *The Little Hump-backed Horse* from a Russian fairytale in 1864. When Arthur Saint-Léon left the Imperial Ballet in 1868 and returned to Paris, the role of ballet master was awarded to the French choreographer Marius Petipa. With Petipa at the helm, Russia once again became the heart of classical ballet internationally. For the next 30 years, he blended the technical Russian accomplishments with the attainments of the Romantic era.

From Perrot, he learned how to pull together a well-prepared *corps de ballet* and from Saint-Léon how to transfer the unique gifts of a ballerina to the ballet. The inspiration of both Perrot and Saint-Léon was significant to Petipa's choreography, *La Bayadère* (1877), *The Sleeping Beauty* (1890), and *Swan Lake* (1895).[13] During his formative years as a dancer, Massine was exposed to this tradition of full-length ballets in Russia, and they were the models for his *The Three-cornered Hat* for the Ballets Russes.

Marius Petipa initiated the tradition of pointe work for all female dancers. Soloists were usually the only performers who danced on pointe. Later, *La Bayadère* became the first ballet that the *corps de ballet* performed wearing pointe shoes. In addition, before he worked in Russia, he danced in Madrid and studied Spanish dance there. He incorporated the steps he learned at the Spanish *escuela bolero* into his choreography.

Petipa is also responsible for developing character dance in the Imperial Ballet School program, after he introduced Russian folk dances in his productions. Character dance became mandatory in the Russian ballet school training program and it is still today.[14] The study of character dance in the ballet curriculum was a part of Massine's early training in Russia, and it would help him attain his expertise in flamenco while the Ballets Russes was in exile in Spain.

As new challenging steps, pointe work, and character dance were added to the curriculum, there were more demands by the school. More rigid physical requirements were imposed for potential candidates and an eight-year program was established.[15] In comparison, flamenco does not have the strict physical requirements of classical ballet because turnout and high extensions are unnecessary. The similarity with the tradition of teachers handing down their knowledge to the next generation of dancers is evident in both flamenco and classical ballet, though the latter also conforms to a graded syllabus.

The length of time for training is different for the two dance forms. Classical ballet usually demands eight years of study, whereas mastering flamenco dance depends on the individual. Another disparity between the two dance forms is the number of years a dancer can perform. While classical ballet dancers have short careers, the flamenco dancer is less limited because there are no extreme physical demands made on the body.

While the French contributed choreographers to the Russian ballet, Italian ballerinas were the principle soloists for the Imperial Ballet. The Italian ballerina, Pierina Legnani from Milano's La Scala, was engaged by Petipa for *Cinderella* in 1893. Her legendary *fouettés* (consecutive turns) en pointe stunned Russian audiences. Legnani shared her secret: strong, hard, box-like pointe shoes, made by the Italian shoemaker, Nicolini. Later, the Russians adapted their own shoes for the purpose of advanced pointe performance. Flamenco dancers would develop their special shoes over time with small nails embedded in the sole and heel. This produced the crisp sound in the dynamic footwork. The shoes evolved from the barefoot kathak origins where small bells attached to the ankle created sound with the movements.

In addition to Italian ballerinas, the great maestro Enrico Cecchetti was invited by Petipa to teach at the Imperial Ballet School.[16] The Italian school was the foundation of the *escuela bolero*, which has an important connection to flamenco. The *fandango* and the *seguidilla* belong to both the *escuela bolero* and flamenco, though as time passes the dances are considered to pertain more to the latter dance form. Both the *fandango* and the *seguidilla* are performed in the ballet *The Three-cornered Hat*.

Composer Peter Tchaikovsky worked with Petipa and became the bridge between Russian heritage and western culture. With the collaboration of Tchaikovsky, the high point in Petipa's artistic life became the ballet *Sleeping Beauty*. The dynamic collaboration of the Russian composer Tchaikovsky with the French choreographer Petipa set a precedent for the Falla and Massine partnership in *Tricorne*.

The addition of more difficult steps called for costume modifications. The Russian *prima ballerina assoluta,* Mathilda Kschessinka, known for her strong technique and dynamic *fouettés,* pioneered the short costume we know today as the tutu. In contrast, flamenco skirts continued to remain the traditional ankle length.[17] The tradition of the *bata de cola,* a flamenco dress with a long, ruffled train, is still used today in performance. While the flamenco costume creates a theatrical effect, it impedes the freedom of movement higher than knee length. *The Three-cornered Hat* costumes offer a compromise. They are shorter than traditional flamenco skirts to accommodate more movement but longer than a tutu in order to retain the Spanish tradition.

Another important groundbreaker was Lev Ivanov, 1834–1901. He is acknowledged with Petipa "for reconciling the Italian and French schools and assisting in forging a characteristic Russian school."[18] Also, he synthesized music and dance in classical ballet, which had always been separate before that time. This unification of music and dance has always been a part of flamenco. Instead of music accompanying dance, it enters the body of the flamenco dancer.

By the end of the 19th century, the Russian Imperial Ballet was one of the greatest companies in the world. While it was built by the French and Italians, the spirit of the Russian dancers drove them to accomplish incredible achievements. The Russian folk dance was strong enough to survive any religious oppression, similar to the survival of the Romani and flamenco. Their history has contributed to their own perseverance. The dance historian Lynn Garafola offers an insight in her *Diaghilev's Ballets Russes.* When Igor Stravinsky said "Certain Andalusian songs remind me of Russian ones,"[19] he was referring to the music and dance of Russia akin to the Spanish, or more precisely Andalusian. But most of all, he was referring to the fire and passion of the soul that both Russians and Spanish have in common when they dance. This important communality would lay the groundwork for the historic collaboration with the Ballets Russes.

Notes

1 Carol Lee, *Ballet in Western Culture, A History of Its Origins and Evolution.* (Needham Heights, MA: Allyn and Bacon, 1999), 182.
2 Ibid., 183.
3 Ibid., 184.
4 Ibid., 186.
5 Ibid., 186.

6 Ibid., 186–7.
7 Ibid., 190.
8 Ibid., 193–4.
9 Ibid., 195.
10 Ibid., 198.
11 Ibid., 202.
12 Ibid., 203.
13 Ibid., 205–7.
14 Ibid., 207.
15 Ibid., 208.
16 Ibid., 209–10.
17 Ibid., 212–4.
18 Ibid., 219.
19 Lynn Garafola, *Diaghilev's Ballets Russes*. (New York and Oxford: Oxford University Press, 1989), 88.

Figure 8.1 The Ballets Russes Company posing for the ballet Sheherazade in the Alhambra Palace, Granada, Spain, 1918. The oriental theme with the exotic background evokes the era when the Moors occupied Spain and later influenced flamenco dance.

8 The Birth of the Ballets Russes

On the threshold of the 20th century, the Russian ballerina, Anna Pavlova, traveled the far ends of the earth, and her performances became a window into the Russian ballet. Slowly, the wonders of Russian art, music, and dance were exposed to world audiences as the new century was heralded in. In the beginning of the 20th century, Russian impresario Serge Diaghilev and his Ballets Russes revolutionized ballet forever. Diaghilev's ballet renaissance would introduce the greatest dancers, choreographers, composers, and designers in history.

The Ballets Russes launched the first productions of *The Firebird, Le Spectre de la Rose,* and *Apollo,* along with *Les Sylphides, Petrouchka,* and many others including *The Three-cornered Hat.* The ballets are still performed around the world today. In addition, Diaghilev launched Russian painting, opera, and music, and he also influenced fashion and design. Undoubtedly, the history of the Ballets Russes and flamenco offers enlightenment into why there were extreme differences in both. Nevertheless, the political turmoil and the onset of the war brought them together and helped contribute to their collaboration.

To understand the creation of the Ballets Russes, it is important first to know about its creator. The dance critic and writer John Percival gives us an understanding of Diaghilev's early years. In his book The World of *Diaghilev,* he wrote that the great impresario was born on March 19, 1872, in the Novgorod province of Russia. Diaghilev's family moved to Perm in 1882 where he developed his love for the arts. In 1890, he was sent to the university to study law and became part of a circle of artists, among them Alexander Benois and Leon Bakst.[1] Along with law, he studied music at the Conservatoire and also became attracted to painting.

In 1896, Diaghilev developed an interest in ballet and published articles on art. When he realized he could influence people, he became a promoter.[2] He wrote in a letter to his stepmother, "I think I have no real gifts. All the same, I think I have just found my true vocation, being a Maecenas."[3] Diaghilev received the title "Russian Maecenas" after the Roman patron of Horace and Virgil.[4]

DOI: 10.4324/9781003366928-8

In 1897, Diaghilev began to organize art exhibits and found backing for his new magazine, *The World of Art*. The magazine reviewed the visual and performing arts and was presented with superior quality to highlight the artwork and illustrations.[5] The magazine closed in 1904 when Diaghilev lost interest in it. He organized a successful exhibit of Russian art in 1905 under the imperial patronage, which led to exhibits in Paris, Berlin, and Vienna. After this success, he organized concerts in Paris with Glazunov, Rachmaninov, and Rimsky-Korsakov.[6] The next step for Diaghilev was to bring the Russian opera to Paris, and Moussorgsky's *Boris Godunov* was the first to be performed in 1908.[7]

Another opera season followed the year after in Paris, and Diaghilev added three short ballets to the program. Though strong in Russia, classical ballet had faded away after the Romantic era in Europe, and the moment was right for the resurgence.[8] He decided to present three ballets by the great choreographer, Michel Fokine, and one of them was *Chopiniana* which was later known as *Les Sylphides*. Another was *Le Pavillon d'Armide*, which was performed in 1907 at the Imperial Theater in Russia. The third ballet, *An Egyptian Night*, was changed to *Cleopatra*. Fokine arranged the dances for the opera *Prince Igor*, and *divertissements* from Petipa's full-length ballets were also presented. With the emphasis on ballet, the Ballets Russes was born and became the most acclaimed company for 20 years.[9]

The Ballets Russes gave its first performance on May 19, 1909, at the Châtelet Theater in Paris. Fokine, Pavlova, and Nijinsky performed the leading roles in all the ballets. Diaghilev generated a rage of excitement and enthusiasm because his productions were superior to anything the public had seen before. "The care taken in preparing and casting his programme was matched by the art with which it was presented to the Parisian public."[10] He cured every detail from redecorating the theater to improving the view of the stage for the audience by removing extra seats.[11] By 1911, the Ballets Russes was working continuously beginning with performances in Monte Carlo, Paris, and their first engagement in London.[12]

Enrico Cecchetti, who had worked for many years in Russia as a ballet teacher, was invited by Diaghilev to teach the company dancers. This was an important step to building the artistic strength of the Ballets Russes and solidifying the high level of technique.[13] When the ballet company opened in London at Covent Garden on June 21, the romantic works of the repertory were more popular with the public. *The Times* of London said, "And above all there is a restraint of emotion. For this is one of the first principles of the art of expressive dancing, that nothing must be taken too seriously .... It is immensely serious as Art, but never for a moment serious as Life."[14]

Nijinsky made his debut as a choreographer with the ballet L'Après-midi d'un Faune. The first performance took place in Paris on May 29, 1912, and the ballet created a scandal. With Diaghilev's increasing promotion of Nijinsky, Fokine made the decision to leave the company.[15] A year later, the

Paris audiences were once again scandalized with Nijinsky's ballet, *The Rite of Spring*, music by Stravinsky.[16] At the first performance, the ballet was met with jeers and mockery from an angry audience. Later, on their South American tour, Diaghilev fired Nijinsky because he failed to show up for his performance in *Carnaval*. But the other reason was because Nijinsky had married while on tour, and it was rumored that Diaghilev had been in love with him.[17]

Michel Fokine was persuaded to return as choreographer for the Ballets Russes. He choreographed the ballet *The Legend of Joseph* in 1914, which introduced a new dancer, Leonide Massine. By the end of the same year, World War I broke out and the company was practically inoperative.[18] However, in 1915, Massine began to successfully choreograph for the company, and one of the ballets was *Parade*, based on a circus theme. It was significant because it introduced modernism and cubism to ballet.[19] During 1917 and 1918, the last two years of the war, the company remained in Spain. With the end of the war, the Ballets Russes opened a season in London. Despite the success of Massine's work, Diaghilev quarreled with him and later fired the choreographer/dancer.[20]

In 1921, Diaghilev produced the ballet *The Sleeping Princess* which was a modified version of Petipa's *The Sleeping Beauty*. He hoped that the production would bring in huge profits, but while the ballet was an artistic success, financially it was not. After Massine had left the Ballets Russes, Nijinsky's sister, Bronislava Nijinska, became the company choreographer. She choreographed the ballet *Les Noces* about a Russian peasant wedding in 1923, and it was a triumph that outlasted time.[21] After Nijinska, Diaghilev tried a new choreographer, George Balanchine. His legacy from the Ballets Russes is the ballet *Apollo* (1928) composed by Stravinsky and *The Prodigal Son* (1929) by Prokofiev.[22] In the summer of 1929, Diaghilev said goodbye to his company for the summer vacation. He died in Venice on August 19, 1929, and was buried there on the island of San Michele.[23]

In the book *The Ballets Russes and its World*, writer/scholar Lynn Garafola and Nancy Van Norman Baer made an astute observation, "Had Serge Diaghilev never lived, it is safe to say 20th century ballet would have been different."[24] Before the advent of the Ballets Russes, classical ballet was stereotyped as exclusively French and Italian. The company demonstrated not only the dynamic Russian technique but also the strikingly unusual beauty of the dancers who intrigued audiences all over the world. Musically and visually Diaghilev's ballets were exciting to the viewer. The great impresario called himself "an incorrigible sensualist."[25]

While Diaghilev once described himself to his stepmother as a man with "no real gifts,"[26] his contributions to the arts were immense. He gave ballet an enormous amount of new music which could harmonically accompany dances or could be enjoyed by ear in a concert hall.[27] "If ballet music today is infinitely more varied and sophisticated than in 1900, it is largely because of Diaghilev."[28] The music of Igor Stravinsky was an example of this idea.

Diaghilev chose to use established painters to design both the ballet scenery and the costumes. This created harmony between the scenery and costumes which was distinguishable because the separate costume and scenery designer became one. This produced a stylistic and artistic coherence inflamed by imagination and genius. Pablo Picasso's contribution to the ballet *Parade* demonstrates this trend in the Ballets Russes productions.[29]

Rebelling against the rules, Diaghilev did not subscribe to the idea of rigid, academic *danse d'école* or the established sequence of the pas de deux formatted by Petipa. Trick steps like *fouetté* turns for the female dancer were rejected by Diaghilev, and while the dancers continued to work on turnout with daily ballet classes, the use of parallel positions became popular with his choreographers. Diaghilev preferred one-act ballets reflected in his choice of *Aurora's Wedding,* or Act III of *Sleeping Beauty,* but he spared nothing in a production and cost was irrelevant.[30]

The Ballets Russes did not have a permanent home in one theater and no star system. [31]The nomadic life of the Ballets Russes resembles that of the Romani pallbearers of Flamenco. Both carried their art on a long journey from home and introduced it to foreign countries. Diaghilev's company had a great impact on flamenco dance and transported it to a theatrical level, but flamenco also enriched the Ballets Russes repertory in its brief exile in Spain.

Notes

1 John Percival, *The World of Diaghilev* (Great Britain: Studio Vista/Dutton Pictureback, 1971) 9–10.
2 Ibid., 12.
3 Ibid., 13.
4 Ibid., 1.
5 Ibid., 13.
6 Ibid., 15.
7 Ibid., 15, 18.
8 Ibid., 18–19.
9 Ibid., 20.
10 Ibid., 27.
11 Ibid., 27.
12 Ibid., 41.
13 Ibid., 42.
14 Ibid., 45.
15 Ibid., 47.
16 Ibid., 48–49.
17 Ibid., 52.
18 Ibid., 52.
19 Ibid., 54.
20 Ibid., 56–57.
21 Ibid., 60.

22 Ibid., 66.
23 Ibid., 68.
24 Lynn Garafola and Nancy Van Norman Baer, *The Ballets Russes and Its World* (New Haven, CT: Yale University Press, 1999), 1.
25 Ibid., 2.
26 Percival, 13.
27 Garafola, 3.
28 Ibid., 4.
29 Ibid.
30 Ibid., 4–6.
31 Ibid., 6.

Figure 9.1 A Flamenco Girl is the title of this photo from 1918. The young woman wears the traditional costume of a flamenco artist and is photographed the same year the Ballets Russes lived in exile in Spain.

9 Leonide Massine and Flamenco in Spain

The choreographer Leonide Massine introduced and established the influence of flamenco in the Ballets Russes. He was born on August 8, 1895, in Moscow and was one of the greatest choreographers of the 20th century. He danced with the Moscow Imperial Theater, especially in character roles, and joined the Ballets Russes in 1913. In 1917, the company remained in exile in Spain during World War I. While traveling in Andalusia, Massine met Félix Fernández García, a famous flamenco dancer who became his teacher. Massine embraced the Spanish culture, which later inspired him to choreograph *The Three-cornered Hat*, a Spanish ballet with flamenco. He brought flamenco to the international stage when the ballet premiered in London on July 22, 1919.

Massine was one of the greatest choreographers of the 20th century and forever associated with Diaghilev's company. The biographer Vicente García-Márquez details the life of the choreographer and dancer in his book *Massine: A Biography*. He wrote that Massine represents a "unifying thread through decades of the development of art in the West" and "an integral part of the cultural history of our century."[1]

Before his career as a choreographer with the Ballets Russes, he was an acclaimed dancer and actor in Russia. It is said that Diaghilev was the influence that encouraged Massine to continue in ballet rather than become an actor.[2] What a huge loss to ballet if he had taken another path and devoted himself to an acting career. Certainly his love of acting would eventually link his destiny to flamenco because an actor must hone into his inner experience to be expressive. Flamenco draws on the internal experience for expression in gestures and movements.

Massine was born on August 8, 1895, in Moscow, and entered the Imperial Theater School of Moscow in 1904. This was around the Petipa and Ivanov period of classical ballet in St. Petersburg. At the time, the director of the Bolshoi was Alexander Gorsky and he favored the dance-drama idea rather than the standard academic ballet.[3] Dancers started to depend on acting for their roles, and this had an impact on Massine who wanted to act more than dance.[4]

DOI: 10.4324/9781003366928-9

In 1905, the school was closed temporarily because of the revolution, and the "Bloody Sunday" massacre would leave a permanent impression on him. The theatrical world of fantasy offered a chance for him to flee from the horrors of war outside his door.[5] At the end of the war, he later wrote in his memoirs: "By the time I was fifteen I had definitely decided that I would be an actor."[6]

Massine continued to dance with the Moscow Imperial Theater, especially in character roles.[7] In addition to dance and drama, he played violin and balalaika in order to understand music better.[8] But it was his friendship with the artist Anatoli Petrovich Bolchakov that had a profound effect on his development. He studied art history and learned how to draw and paint, which added more depth to his inner artistic experience.[9] Another great influence in his life was the Russian drama master, Konstantin Stanislavsky, who through his teachings guided Massine in his character and dramatic roles.[10] In August of 1912, Massine graduated and was accepted into the Bolshoi Ballet.[11]

Serge Diaghilev discovered Massine while he danced with the Bolshoi Theater in 1913. He was looking for the perfect dancer to perform the role of Joseph in *The Legend of Joseph*, a biblical ballet that would be choreographed by Fokine. Diaghilev was impressed by his performances in *Swan Lake* and *Don Quixote*.[12] Massine was thrilled to be offered a contract to join the Ballets Russes and left Moscow with Diaghilev for Europe.

Massine and Diaghilev met the company in Germany, and before he worked on *The Legend of Joseph*, he performed in Fokine's *Petrouchka*. Massine admired Fokine and was influenced by his choreography. He was fascinated by Fokine's talent in mixing dance, music, drama, and painting, which the ballet *Petrouchka* exemplified.[13]

When World War I was declared in 1914, the Ballets Russes was in Paris. For two years, the company continued to tour Europe and the United States, but in 1916, they arrived on the shores of Spain. King Alfonso XIII invited the Ballets Russes to perform at Madrid's Teatro Real. They arrived by boat at the port city of Cádiz, where centuries before the first dancers from the Middle East disembarked. The composer Manuel de Falla took the company sightseeing and introduced them to flamenco dance and music. Cádiz captivated Massine and Andalusia left an impression on him. This was an inspirational moment that lead to his eventual masterpiece, *The Three-cornered Hat*.[14]

The pandemonium of the war brought together great artists, and the osmosis of new artistic ideas was bonded. From Cádiz the Ballets Russes journeyed to Madrid for their opening on May 26, 1917, at the Teatro Real. Madrid was immune to the war in Europe, so "aristocrats, millionaires, artists, and swindlers all compounded the intrigue."[15] Talented artists had escaped from their war-torn countries, and as a result, the quality of the arts and cultural manifestations was at a high level. The meeting of classical ballet with flamenco began with the advent of World War I, when the nomadic Ballets Russes was invited to remain under the protection of Spain's King Alfonso.

The tour of the Spanish peninsula became a productive and creative detour for the company which formed important liaisons. Massine was awed by the El Escoriol outside of Madrid, and he wrote to Anatoli Petrovich "In some parts there is the simplicity of Byzantium and everywhere there is powerful spirit and mighty form."[16] Massine also wrote "We are all crazy about what we see at the Prado."[17] While performing at the Teatro Real in Madrid, he frequented the Prado museum where Goya inspired his choreographic designs along with Velásquez.

Besides learning a new dance form, his passion for Spanish art profoundly influenced his work and overflowed into his choreography. The paintings of Goya shaped his choreography, but the style of Velásquez intrigued him and subsequently affected his ballets.[18] Velázquez's *Las Meninas* moved him deeply, and with Diaghilev's suggestion, he choreographed a ballet. The ballet *Las Meninas*, with the music *Pavane* by Fauré, was created in honor of the painter Velásquez.[19] Massine wrote in his memoir "Through my study of Spanish music and the paintings of El Greco, Goya, Ribera, and Velasquez, I had widened my understanding of the dignity and passion of the Spanish temperament."[20]

When the Madrid engagement was over, Diaghilev, Massine, and Falla visited the cities of Andalusia. In Seville, Massine saw the Gothic Cathedral and was amazed by "the altar dances with castanets, and the orchestra in front of the altar." He was referring to the flamenco *mesas* in Spanish churches. While traveling in Andalusia, the three men met the flamenco dancer Félix Fernández García in the famous Café Novedades, and later he became Massine's flamenco teacher.[21]

Massine, Diaghilev, and Falla continued on to Granada, where they were captivated by its magical beauty. Again, Massine wrote to Anatoli Petrovich when he saw the Alhambra "I saw a miracle, or was it a wonderful, uncommon dream?[22] Later the company performed the ballet *Scheherazade* in the garden of the Alhambra. At the same time, flamenco flourished in the Romani caves of Granada and the proximity of both set the stage for the meeting of the two dance forms. Massine attended Romani banquets, one in Albaicín, the old Arabic town, and he learned more and more about the Romani traditions.[23]

Manuel de Falla was interested in making the Andalusian *canto jondo*, emotional songs that often accompany flamenco dance, popular again.[24] Before the trip, Falla composed music for the theatrical company Martínez Síerras. He composed *El amor brujo* for the famous flamenco *bailaora*, Pastora Imperio, who worked with the theatrical company. Also, Falla was composing music for the pantomime *El Corregidor y la molinera* for the Martínez Síerras group. He offered to make *El Corregidor y la molinera* into a ballet, which is based on the Spanish novel *El Sombrero de tres picos* by Pedro Antonio de Alarcón.[25]

After their trip to Andalusia, Falla was inspired to change parts of *El Corregidor* and to adapt the music more to the dances.[26] Falla studied Spanish folk dancing and music in order to interpret certain dances, such as the *farruca*, in a modern idiom.[27] Massine wrote in his memoir *My Life in Ballet* "Falla's score, with its pulsating rhythms, played by eleven brass instruments, seemed to us very exciting, and its blend of violence and passion was similar to much of the music of the local folk dances."[28]

Diaghilev and Massine met Félix Fernández García in Madrid where he was dancing in a café. Diaghilev offered him a contract to join the company before leaving for Barcelona.[29] In Barcelona, Fernández García began to teach Massine Flamenco steps and introduced him to his teacher who taught him the difficult *zapateado*. Diaghilev, Falla, and Massine repeated the trip they had made the year before in Andalusia, and this time Fernández García joined them. They picked up bits and pieces of music and dance blending this into a new form.

In Seville, Massine met and filmed the famous flamenco dancers, Ramírez and Macarrona, and he described their dancing as "ferocious power and elegance." In their travels, Falla listened to a blind man play the guitar in the streets of Grenada and he hummed the melody until he could write it down.[30] Massine wrote in his memoir "He [Falla] later used that melody for the *sevillana* in the second part of our ballet, which we finally entitled the *Tricorne*"[31] or *The Three-cornered Hat*. Massine felt he was almost ready to choreograph a Spanish ballet with flamenco, Spanish folk dances, and with the influence of classical ballet, its style, and choreographic techniques.

Massine returned to Barcelona where he said, "I filled my time by going to watch bullfights, to which I became addicted."[32] He discovered that the elegant movements of the bullfighter were as perfect as those of the great flamenco dancers. The term *tauromaquia* refers to the art of bullfighting and the dance technique it inspires. He declared, "I began to grasp the underlying ferocity present in such dances as the *farruca*." He added, "I realized too that it was essentially the same elements in the Spanish temperament which had produced both dances and their national sport."[33]

Falla arrived in Barcelona with the completed score of *The Three-cornered Hat*, and at the same time Pablo Picasso had begun the designs for costumes and scenery.[34] The composer underlined his goal, "to capture the mood, rhythm, melodic forms, and cadences, but eschewed the perpetuation of the literal popular form, opting instead to try for a personal and original interpretation."[35] Massine who was always the actor before the dancer had a strong relationship with character styles of movement. The Spanish dance idiom in *The Three-cornered Hat* is one of his most successful depictions. He incorporated components from the circus, commedia dell'arte, film, folklore, cultural traditions, and the idioms of modernism.[36]

Tamara Karsavina danced the role of the Miller's wife and Massine danced the role of the Miller. He had decided to dance the part rather than Félix Fernández García because like most flamenco dancers, Félix's work was improvisational. This was a great disappointment for Fernández García because he had taught Massine flamenco but did not have a part in the ballet.[37]

Karsavina was amazed at Massine's Spanish dancing and commented, "On the Russian stage we had been used to the balletic stylization of Spanish dancing, sugary at its best, but this was the very essence of Spanish folk dancing."[38] In the *Tricorne* pas de deux, Massine described his interpretation "I tried to achieve that quality of pursuit, of tension, teasing, advancing and retreating, which is a salient feature of so many Spanish dances."[39]

Massine also wrote about his choreography "Although the dance was mainly inspired by the *fandango* and with some *flamenco* passages, I added to it a variety of classical movements."[40] The whole cast of dancers joined in a *jota* finale. This was the collaboration of Falla's music, Picasso's costumes and scenery, along with Massine's choreography, all sewn together by the inspirational thread of the painter Goya's life and work.[41]

The Three-cornered Hat, or *Tricorne*, did not premiere in Spain but opened in London on July 22, 1919. Paradoxically, the name of the theater was the Alhambra. The ballet is the synthesis of classical movements, Spanish folk dance, and flamenco. Massine artfully incorporated his own expression into the *farruca*, the *fandango*, the *sevillana*, and the *jota*, without compromising the qualities and elements of each dance form.[42] Massine used the dynamics of flamenco and Spanish dancing, which is the increasing and decreasing of speed exemplified in the *farruca*. Also, he set the mood by using choreographic tools such as tension, provocation, and advancing, retreating movements common in Spanish dance.[43] This new genre is often referred to as modern folk character ballet. However, the *farruca* and the *fandango* pertain to flamenco dance and therefore belong to a separate category within the genre.[44]

Notes

1. Vicente García-Márquez, *Massine: A Biography*. (New York: Knopf, 1995), xiii.
2. John Percival, *The World of Diaghilev*. (Great Britain: Studio Vista/ Dutton Pictureback, 1971), 80.
3. García-Márquez, 9.
4. Ibid., 10.
5. Ibid., 11.
6. Ibid., 17.
7. Ibid., 18.
8. Ibid., 17.
9. Ibid., 21.
10. Ibid., 24–25.
11. Ibid., 21.
12. Ibid., 31.
13. Ibid., 35.
14. Ibid., 67–68.
15. Ibid., 68.
16. Ibid., 70.
17. Ibid., 71.
18. Ibid., 71.
19. Ibid., 75.
20. Leonide Massine, *My Life in Ballet*. (London: Macmillan, 1968), 118–9.

21 García-Márquez, 72.
22 Ibid., 73.
23 Ibid., 73.
24 Ibid., 72.
25 Ibid., 107–8.
26 Ibid., 73–74.
27 Massine, 115.
28 Ibid., 115.
29 García-Márquez, 109.
30 Ibid., 112.
31 Massine, 118.
32 Ibid., 122.
33 Ibid., 122.
34 Ibid., 122.
35 García-Márquez, 113.
36 Lynn Garafola and Nancy Van Norman Baer, *The Ballets Russes and Its World.* (New Haven, CT: Yale University Press, 1999), 257.
37 García-Márquez, 131–2.
38 Ibid., 132.
39 Massine, 141.
40 Ibid., 141.
41 García-Márquez, 138.
42 Ibid., 138.
43 Ibid., 138.
44 Ibid., 138.

10 Flamenco's Contrasts and Similarities to Other Dance Forms

Character Dance and the Bolero School

Character dance is considered a branch of classical ballet and an essential part of the classical repertory. In character dance, the traditions of dance in different nations are adapted to ballet for theatrical purposes. The word "character" suggests the portrayal of the attributes that belong to a particular individual or nation and combined with the local dance styles. The steps and styles must be analyzed to fully understand the characteristics of each nationality. Some examples of character dance include the czardas, mazurka, polka, tarantella, and flamenco used in classical ballet to depict the place or country in the narrative of a ballet.

The dancer, choreographer, and writer Jurgen Pagels wrote a detailed book on the subject *Character Dance*. He observed that often various steps and national folk dance styles are mixed together and the authenticity is lost. Choreographers try to avoid this assimilation.[1] However, many dance forms were assimilated to create the art of flamenco. Here is a comparison and contrast with flamenco dance and character dance including the history and training methods of both dance forms.

In Spain, there are three main styles of Spanish dance. One is regional and usually featured in open air festivals. The traditional folk dance of each region requires attention on the part of the dancer to preserve detail and character. Spanish classical dance is another style and is a form of 18th-century Italian ballet. It was popular in the 19th century and continues to be performed on stage or in a *tablao*. The third style is flamenco, with ancient roots in kathak Indian dance. Today, flamenco is performed in theatrical venues, the *tablao*, which is a typical flamenco show, and in the caves of Granada for tourists.

There is no single country that represents character dance. Hungary, Russia, Poland, and other eastern European countries contribute to character dance, along with Italy and Spain. The national dances have not absorbed a cultural transformation on a long voyage as flamenco experienced. Character dance became popular all over Europe and was not isolated to one place. It was performed in many of the most famous ballets in the late 1800s. One of the earliest was *Coppélia*, later *Swan Lake*, the *Nutcracker*, and *Don Quixote*, which exemplified classical Spanish dancing. Character dance has also appeared in

DOI: 10.4324/9781003366928-10

operas, operettas, and musicals, whereas flamenco has been more limited in range because of exclusivity to one region.

A ballet dancer seeking a professional career needs to know character as part of the necessary performance skills. Usually dancers from a classical background have an easier time adapting to the dance form than those coming from other disciplines. But classically trained dancers often have difficulty with character and flamenco because of the posture and placement. Flamenco dancers must always work with slightly bent knees or in *demi-plié*, a similarity with character dance. But the difference lies in the finish: character dance finishes a combination or dance with straight knees, whereas flamenco ends in demi-plié. However, it should be noted that prior character training can facilitate the study of flamenco, especially for ballet dancers.

Another comparison is the position of the spine. The shoulders are pulled back and the spine is extremely arched, which is the typical posture of Andalusian and flamenco dance. One of my teachers utilized a stick for upper body stretching, which helped with the arms that are positioned behind the head and back twists or *torcido*. Character follows the upper body rules of classical ballet, which is the rib-cage lifted, the spine straight, and the *épaulement,* or use of the shoulders, emphasized.

The pelvis swivels in flamenco especially in the figure eight design of the *rumba gitana,* whereas the hips are squarely placed in character and classical ballet. The flamenco skirt is usually worn tighter to impede broad leg movements. This was the result of the Muslim belief dictating that a woman's legs should not be seen. In all three dance forms, character, classical ballet, and flamenco, the torso moves circularly and freely with the sweeping shape of the arms.

The contrast with the hand shapes and movements in the two disciplines is noteworthy. Here the character dance again follows the rules of classical ballet along with palms turned upward and extended fingers. In flamenco, the fingers create various shapes which distinguish the hands. Almost all my flamenco teachers work extensively on exercises to articulate the beautiful hand movements of flamenco. It is interesting to note that the arm positions in flamenco are similar to classical ballet, though the hands are articulated differently.

There are two additional arm positions in Spanish dancing and flamenco: fourth back with one arm placed behind the back and fifth low (*en bas*) behind the back. *En bas* is the same in character and flamenco, and *en avant, a la seconde,* and *en haut* have palms open. Castanets are used in character but rarely in flamenco, though there is hand clapping in both dance forms.

Character training begins at the *barre* with a series of exercises that follow a similar lesson plan to classical ballet. After the warm-up at the *barre,* the class proceeds with center work.[2] Flamenco has no set exercises, syllabus, sequence of set steps, or *barre,* so the structure of the class depends totally on the teacher. Steps have been passed down to each generation from families and teachers. Unfortunately, nothing was ever written, so many of the steps and dances were lost over the years as a result of not being codified.

A typical flamenco class will begin with footwork and proceed to the teacher's choreography for the lesson. One striking difference in the comparison of character and flamenco is music. Character dance works with musical counts of 6 and 8, but flamenco uses 12 counts. Both character and flamenco have a few of the same positions of the feet as ballet with the sixth position or parallel. There is an addition of an open fourth in character and a *planta natural* or relaxed third position in flamenco. The shoes in both dance styles look the same on the surface, but flamenco has rough, nail-like metal spikes on the heels and upper sole.

Ballet and character are extroverted in emotion, light, outward in movement, and spatially cover wide open distances. Flamenco is introverted. The emotion erupts and simmers internally, but the space around the dancer remains tight. The character dancer brings their artistry to the story that accompanies the ballet they are performing. The flamenco dancer performs to a theme story of life which can be happy or sad. It is their individual story. The human emotions are felt deeply and come forth in the interpretation of the performer.

The dances have names according to their mood, but every teacher choreographs their own interpretation. The *alegrías* is a dance for joy and happiness which came out of the Romani quarter of Cadiz and is the preferred by flamenco dancers.[3] The *bulerias* signifies laughter, joking, mockery, and the Romani of Jerez specialized in this dance, which is often added to the end of the *alegrías*. The *soleares* represents solitude, loneliness, and a touch of sadness and is difficult to master until the dancer understands the refrain in the music reflecting the steps. When some *escuelo bolero* steps are added, these dances become more interesting and challenging. While unusual, the addition demonstrates the compatibility of the two dance forms together in choreography.

The soul of flamenco is called *duende*, and without it, the audience does not become involved in the performance but merely entertained. The dancer and writer Matteo Marcellus Vittucci describes *duende* as "Fundamentally speaking, *duende* is a state of mind or emotion emanating from the subconscious, an imperceptible psychic communication or hypnotic energy which a performer shares with his or her audience."[4] The dancer almost seems "possessed" with a fire of emotion that comes forth in a so-called dance ritual.

Diaghilev's Ballets Russes was instrumental in bringing character dance to the western world from 1909 to 1929 when the company dominated the stage. The success of the character Polovtsian Dances in *Prince Igor* resulted in the birth of one of the greatest ballet companies in history.[5] Leonide Massine studied flamenco while the company was in exile in Spain, and his experience with character dance helped him to easily adapt to flamenco. Character was helpful in the study of flamenco's footwork because usually ballet dancers without this particular training have difficulty. Ballet dancers are taught not to make a sound with their feet.

Massine used his experience with character dance, classical ballet, and flamenco to choreograph the ballet *The Three-cornered Hat* in 1918 for the Ballets Russes and perform the famous "Miller's Dance." In order to understand the choreographers' process of study which helped him to create the ballet, I studied flamenco. The footwork is similar to tap dance. For example, the *golpe* is similar to the *stomp.* The knees are bent in flamenco as they are in character, which I was prepared for after studying ballroom. The anomaly in flamenco is working with music in twelve *compas* instead of the usual eight counts in classical ballet.

Marina Grut, President of the Spanish Dance Society and writer for the *Flamenco International Magazine*, gives an extensive, reliable resource in her book *The Bolero School.* According to the writer, *escuelo bolera*, or the bolero school, has origins similar to classical ballet and a path much different from flamenco. Similarities with the Cecchetti Method of classical ballet are visible in the bolero school, along with the Bournonville or Danish style of ballet. The Bournonville style is similar to the 19th-century French balletic style which was part of the same period of history as the Spanish classical dance. The bolero school combined the Italian and French ballet with regional Spanish dance. In the 18th century, classical bolero like classical ballet was presented in the theater, and in the 19th century, the bolero became Spain's "national dance."

Spanish folk dance, especially from Andalusia, strongly influenced the bolero school and flamenco. For this reason, there is often confusion in identifying one dance form from the other because they both share steps from Spanish folk dances.[6] While the boundaries between popular Spanish dance and pure flamenco are sometimes unclear, the style of the two dance forms is different. However, some teachers are very clear about the border dividing flamenco from the *escuela bolera.* Others mix both dance forms in a class. Whether separate or combined, it is necessary to focus on the upper part of the body and the diverse hand shapes used in flamenco. Years of ballet training help upper body movements, but footwork can be a challenge.

Marina Grut wrote in *The Bolero School* "Spanish dancing is such a vital force, it could not but have influenced ballet."[7] There is evidence that Spanish dance influenced classical ballet. Arm positions and *épaulement* always existed in Spanish dancing before classical ballet. An example of similarities is the "shared inheritance" with Cecchetti's *pas de bourrée couru* and the bolero school *piffa y pas de bourrée.* The ballet step *pas de basque* belongs to the syllabus of the *escuela bolera* and came from a regional Spanish dance.

Contrary to what many think, Spanish dance is not ballet with castanets. A ballet dancer would need extra study to accomplish difficult jumps while performing with castanets.[8] Flamenco dancers almost never use castanets in their repertory. In Spanish dance, the *zapatilla,* or ballet slippers, are the primary shoes used for dancing because of the high and difficult jumps executed. When the bolero is performed in a theatrical venue, the female dancer often wears pointe shoes. However, there are dances that use the flamenco shoe, particularly those with the *golpe punta y talon*.

The *sevillanas* in the *escuela bolera* comes from an Andalusian folk dance. However, the *sevillanas* is associated more and more with flamenco because of its connection with Andalusia. Here is an example where the three dance forms, bolero, folk, and flamenco, became mixed together.[9] The *sevillanas* chorus step was used by the ballet choreographers like Bournonville in his Spanish ballet, *Seguidilla*, and Petipa in *Don Quixote*. Later, the step was used by Massine in the Dance of the Neighbors in *The Three-cornered Hat*.

The posture of the back in the *sevillanas* interpreted by classical ballet choreographers was swayed, perhaps a reflection of the matador stance or an exaggeration for theatrical purposes. But according to the bolero school, the sway back position was misunderstood by ballet choreographers.[10] Bolero dancers who perform the *sevillanas* have very straight backs to support the technical difficulties that challenge them in other steps.[11]

In the early 19th century, the Escuela Bolera Andaluza in Cádiz incorporated flamenco with the bolero. The flamenco *alegrías* and *soleares* were performed in a classical style. "The local dance masters seem to have created these dances for their studios from the street forms."[12] Spanish dance became recognized after 1833, especially on the stages of London and Paris during the Romantic period. In 1834, the first Spanish dance company was acclaimed on the stage of the Paris Opera. The curvaceous sexuality of the Spanish dancer was a stark contrast to the fragile, cold French ballerina.

Flamenco dancers were also heavier because they did not follow the rigid body requirements of classical ballet. In Paris, Théophile Gautier, French critic, writer, and proponent of romanticism, commented on Spanish dance, comparing it to the French ballet:

> The Spanish dancers, although they lack the polish, the requisite correctness and the elevation of the French are, in my view, far superior to them in grace an enchantment. As they work little and do not submit themselves to those exercises in agility that make a dance class a torture chamber, they avoid the leanness of a trained horse that gives our dances a macabre and excessively anatomical aspect; they preserve the curves and roundness of their sex; *they look like women who dance rather than like ballerinas,* which is completely different. Their way of dancing has not the faintest similarity to the French School.[13]

Spanish regional dancing, flamenco, and bolero have something in common: shouting and hand clapping which is called *jaleo*.[14] In contrast to flamenco, female dancers performing the bolero wear much shorter skirts to accommodate more movement, especially jumps. Both flamenco and the bolero steps and movements were handed down from generation to generation. However, in the late 19th century, Angel Pericet Carmona created a graded curriculum based on the steps and movements that he inherited from his family.[15] The Pericet system is studied worldwide, whereas flamenco academies to this day have no graded curriculum.

The popularity of Spanish dance began to decline around 1860, around the same time the Romantic Era in classical ballet was coming to an end. In the early 20th century, flamenco and bolero were performed together on the *tablao* or stage. The *cuadro* or picture contained a group of dancers and musicians working together. The classical *cuadro* flamenco performed the first part of the show, and the *cuadro* bolero danced in the second half.[16]

Notes

1 Jurgen Pagels, *Character Dance* (Bloomington: Indiana University Press, 1984), 1.
2 Ibid., 3.
3 Matteo Marcellus Vittucci, *The Language of Spanish Dance, A Dictionary and Reference Manual*. 2nd ed. (Hightstown, NJ: Princeton Book Company, 2003), 14.
4 Ibid., 74.
5 Pagels, 2.
6 Marina Grut, *The Bolero School* (England: Dance Books, 2002), 6.
7 Ibid.
8 Ibid., 7.
9 Ibid., 25.
10 Ibid., 7.
11 Ibid., 7.
12 Ibid., 111.
13 Gerhard Steingress, *Antecedents of Carmen in the History of Spanish Dance*, page 121. K.Meira Goldberg, Ninotchka Devorah Bennahum, and Michelle Heffner Hayes. *Flamenco on the Global Stage, Historical, Critical, and Theoretical Perspectives*. McFarland & Company, Jefferson, North Carolina. 2015
14 Matteo Marcellus Vittucci, The Language of Spanish Dance, 121.
15 Ibid., 80.
16 Grut, 52.

11 Two Flamenco Dances

The *Fandango* and
The *Farruca*

According to Carlo Blasis, the Italian master of dance and scholar who wrote *The Code of Terpsichore* in 1728, the word *fandango* means "Go and dance." However, his definition is disputable in some circles. The dance is considered to be very old, and experts claim it is possible that it dates back to the Phoenicians, around 1600 B.C. Of all Spanish dances, it is thought to be the most Spanish, danced by all social classes on all occasions, and performed by couples or individuals. "The *fandango*, however, was so thoroughly naturalized in Spain, that every Spaniard may be said to be born with it in his head and heels."[1]

The *fandango* is danced in every region of Spain in some form or other. Different forms are named after their city of inception in Andalusia. For example, the *malagueña* is named after the city of Málaga, *granadina* for Granada, *murciana* for Murcia, *rodeña* for Ronda, and *fandango* de Huelva for Huelva. It resembles a *fiesta* of dance and music, and the exciting rhythm, repetitious in nature, often accelerates with the sound of castanets. The merrymaking climaxes in a wild frenzy of music and dance.

The *fandango* is thought of as flamenco but transcended from folkloric dance. In the beginning, the common folk danced it at street festivals, churches, cafes, courts, salons, and parties. In addition to castanets, they used tambourines and violins for music. *Fandangos* are often danced in heels or hemp-soled sandals called *alpargatas*. They are considered regional dances from Andalusia, but a classical interpretation of the dances has been created as it was for the *bolero*. *Fandangos* were couple dances used for courtship. However, in the south of Spain, the domination of the Moors produced a dance trio, one man and two women. Recently, the dance is performed as a solo interpretation in concert productions in theaters.[2]

Casanova, 1725, wrote about seeing the electrifying *fandango* during a theater performance in Madrid. The *fandango*, like many dances all over Europe, was inserted between acts in theatrical productions. Doña Pichona was Casanova's escort at that performance, and she revealed to him that the Romani were the best *fandango* dancers. This idea was unanimous in Europe.

DOI: 10.4324/9781003366928-11

The next day he hired a Roma dance teacher and added the *fandango* to his variety of seduction methods.³

In 1775, the British writer Richard Twiss observed Spanish dance on different occasions in Madrid. He said, "There were two types of *fandango*, one decent and the other 'gallant.'"⁴ The Vatican wanted to ban the *fandango*, and the dance was judged by a panel of their Eminences. Two dancers were chosen to demonstrate for the Fathers. The merriment and elegance of the dance impressed the holy judges, and the dance was approved and returned to its popular status in Spain.⁵ An old Spanish proverb declares, "This world is a *fandango*, and he who does not dance is a fool."⁶

The *Farruca*

The *farruca* is a dance which "embodies all the technique of the other flamenco dances." The name of the dance originates from a song brought south to Andalusia by workers from Galicia, Spain. The meaning of the word *farruca* is debated. Some authorities say it is the bagpipe used in the northwestern province of Galicia, and some say it is the name of the song. Others say it is used to describe the northerners from Asturias and Galicia, along with the adjectives "brave" and "courageous."

Flamenco music has roots in Andalusia, so the *farruca* was adopted into the art form because of musical similarity and its ability to adapt. However, it is different from other flamenco dances because it can be performed without singers. In the late nineteenth century, the Spanish musician Ramon Montoya introduced *farruca* music on the guitar. A *gitano* dancer from Andalusia created dance steps and movements to the *farruca* music. El Faico was the flamenco dancer from Triana Seville who introduced the dance in Andalusia.

The *farucca* is usually danced by a man, but women have also performed the dance. Women wear riding habits or trousers with a high waist, *pantalones cenidos*.⁷ The *farruca* does not send an emotional message, describe the pain of the Romani, or the story of the assimilation of steps and movements on a long journey across centuries and countries by a group of nomads. It is simply dancing and is appreciated for its technical virtuosity.

The *caída* and the *vuelta quebradita* are two awe-inspiring movements performed in the *farruca*. The *paso de caída* is a falling or dropping step onto the knees, usually preceded by a rapid turn (*vuelta*). The "timing is flexible and it can be used for punctuation within a dance by reversing the action. The fall comes first, followed by a sudden spring to a vertical position on the balls of the feet, which is accented on the second count."⁸ Usually, the step is performed by lifting up the ball of the right foot, similar to a ballet *relevé*. The left leg is bent with the left foot touching the knee resembling a ballet *passé* with the leg turned in or the stork position. The arms are in a low fourth position, and the body is arched in a slight *cambré*. The dancer lunges forward onto the right knee with the left leg bent. Female dancers use a slower *caída* and a slow, circular *vuelta* to their knees, permitting the flamenco *bata de cola* to form a dramatic circle on the floor around the dancer's kneeling body.[9]

The *vuelta quebradita*, or small, broken, fractured turn, is a turn performed with a half-circle backbend. The footwork resembles the *soutenu* in classical ballet. The arms are in fourth position with the left arm up and the right foot front in third position. The torso bends to the left and the ball of the left foot crosses over the right foot. At the same time, the arms change position after passing through first position. Turning right on the balls of the feet, the arms pass in front of the face and change back to the original position. A backbend is made on the turn and the body is inclined over the right thigh.[10] The *paseo de farruca* is the promenade or walk in the *farruca* used in the more melancholic phrases of music. In addition, the stance of the bullfighter can be seen in many final poses.

The *farruca* is in a 2/4 signature, and only two other flamenco dances have this tempo: the *tango* and the *garrotín*. The majority of flamenco dances are in the 3/4 and 3/8 time. The *tiempo de farruca* is defined as time marked to the *farruca* rhythm and the name of the step that marks the time. This "time-marking step" is performed in the beginning of the *farruca* or during more difficult versions of the dance. Again, the arms are placed in a low fourth position with the left arm front and the feet are parallel. The ball of the right foot beats the floor on the first count. On the second count, the same leg extends forward close to the floor. The ball of the right foot steps slightly back, with knee relaxed, and the left foot steps back and joins the right on count four. The step moves backward, but the body is always kept at the same level. The fingers snap to the rhythm, and this is defined as *pitos*.[11]

The *zapateado*, or the dance rhythms made with shoes, defines the essence of all flamenco. The dancer uses this technique with any part of the *zapato*, or shoe, to make "rhythmic and counter rhythmic patterns." This includes stamps, soft brushing steps, heel beats, and any toe-heel combinations that the dancer can create with his shoes to produce sounds.[12] In the *farruca*, the footwork is very strong and balances the dynamic leaps, turns, and falls that belong to this particular flamenco dance. The *contratiempo*, which means against time or count, is produced on the offbeat or between the beats and creates an exciting effect.[13]

The *remachos* describes the sounds or rhythmic pattern performed in the *farruca*. "Its name comes from the hammering action of the lower leg, as though it were pounding a nail down firmly."[14] The *remachos* begins in a third position with the left foot front or parallel feet facing toward stage right. The dancer looks to the audience in both preparations and knees are slightly bent. The step is executed in place and usually performed at the end of the dance. A syncopated small hop on the left foot launches the step, lifting lower right leg back from knee. The first three counts is a stamp of the right foot, and the third stamp is accented with a hold on count four. This entire sequence is repeated three times consecutively and rapidly.[15]

The first visual example of the *farruca* preserved on film was made more than 100 years ago. In 1917, while dancing with the Ballets Russes, Leonide Massine filmed the *Spanish Dancers*. This film is thought to be one of the most important treasures of flamenco contained at the New York Public Library for the Performing Arts. The first part was filmed in the street and the second part on a rooftop, both backgrounds in Seville, Spain. The first part is profound and an excellent documentary to the legendary flamenco *bailaora*, La Macarrona, but the second part of the film demonstrates the *farruca*.

The *bailaor* in this part is the famous flamenco dancer Ramírez, and he performs the *farruca*. Here we see exactly what Massine visualized through the camera lens. He concentrated on the body from the ankle up but surprisingly did not film the footwork. The dancing is more technical, the turns and jumps resembling character dance, instead of flamenco as we know it. This seemed unusual at the time that I first viewed the film, but later this phenomenon was explainable. Flamenco has absorbed traditional Spanish folk dances, so this applies to what appears to be the element of character dance in the *farruca*. The body curve of Ramírez is highlighted in the film, and it reflects the proud stance of the bullfighter that Massine had studied.

After viewing this film, I observed and studied the *farruca* choreographed for the Miller's Dance in the ballet *The Three-cornered Hat*. I viewed the original 1937 film of *The Three-cornered Hat*, with Massine and Toumanova, at the New York Public Library for the Performing Arts with the permission of the Massine family. The film reflects much of what the choreographer learned from the Vargas film. Tatiana Massine suggested that I watch another film in which her father performed the *farruca*. It contained steps from the *farruca* he performed in the Miller's Dance in *The Three-cornered Hat*. After watching both films, I was glad for this suggestion because the 1937 version was of poor quality and difficult to see clearly.

The black and white 1937 movie contained other Spanish dances, but the *farruca* and the *fandango* are the only dances that belong to flamenco. In Massine's solo film, there was a stunning similarity to the second part of the *Spanish Dances* with the dancer Ramírez. However, the *farruca* has a limited amount of specific steps which is the reason why the steps are repeated. As mentioned before, flamenco has no set step patterns or written composition because it was handed down from generation to generation, usually by family members.

Massine's performance was elegant but resembled ballet with its external energy. The *farruca* is one flamenco dance that is more theatrical and less internal. Flamenco has a heavy connection with the earth, but the *farruca* uses the earth as a springboard like classical ballet. Also, the energy of flamenco dance smolders internally unlike the *farruca* that dissipates externally. Massine's body curve repeats the stance of the bullfighter which he admired so much.[16] At first, it seems that Massine is imitating Spanish dancing with ballet, but after close observation, it is evident that his interpretation of the *farruca* is authentic.

Notes

1. Lou Charnon-Deutsch, *The Spanish Gypsy, The History of a European Obsession* (University Park: The Pennsylvania State University Press, 2004), 50.
2. Matteo Marcellus Vittucci, *The Language of Spanish Dance, A Dictionary and Reference Manual*. 2nd ed. (Hightstown, NJ: Princeton Book Company, 2003), 50.
3. Charnon-Deutsch, 50.
4. Ibid., 92.
5. Vittucci, 84.
6. Ibid., 84.
7. Ibid., 85–86.
8. Ibid., 158.
9. Ibid., 44.
10. Ibid., 262–3.
11. Ibid., 237.
12. Ibid., 267.
13. Ibid., 60.
14. Ibid., 209.
15. Ibid., 210.
16. Leonide Massine, *My Life in Ballet* (London: Macmillan, 1968), 122.

Figure 12.1 Leonide Massine and Tamara Karsavina photographed for *The Three-cornered Hat* ballet in 1919.

Source: Photo contributed by Leo Boudreau.

12 Analysis of the *Miller's Dance* and *The Three-cornered Hat* Story

Massine's one-act ballet, *The Three-cornered Hat,* successfully premiered at the Alhambra Theater in London, England, on July 22, 1919. The music was composed by Manuel de Falla, and the scenery and costumes were designed by Pablo Picasso. The union of flamenco and classical ballet is observed in Massine's ballet, which has survived the passage of time and is still performed by companies today. A synopsis of *The Three-cornered Hat* is recounted in the book by George Balanchine and Francis Mason, *101 Stories of the Great Ballets,* and is imperative to understanding the context of the dance.

The ballet tells of a Spanish love story in a small village in Spain, and the scene opens with the miller and his wife. The governor of the province, or *Corregidor*, arrives with an escort. He is dressed in fine clothes and wearing a three-cornered hat, which is a sign of his position, class, and power. The old *Corregidor* flirts with the miller's wife, but she ignores him and he departs. Here she dances a lively *fandango*. The *Corregidor* returns and continues to pursue her, but she pushes him away and he falls. The miller with his wife help the *Corregidor* to his feet. But the angry dignitary threatens both of them before leaving the scene. The miller and his wife perform a pas de deux.[1]

Evening comes and the villagers dance the *seguidillas* in a festival with the miller and his wife. After drinking and celebrating, the miller performs the famous *farruca*. Soldiers sent by the *Corregidor* come and arrest him. With the miller gone, the *Corregidor* continues to pursue his wife until she pushes him in the river. The miller escapes and takes the *Corregidor's* drying clothes and wears them. The *Corregidor* has borrowed the miller's dry clothes, and he is arrested because of mistaken identity. When the villagers find out what the *Corregidor* tried to do, they drive him out of the village. The *jota* is performed by the villagers along with the miller and his wife as a victory dance. A dummy representing the *Corregidor* is thrown in the air above the crowd as the curtain falls.[2]

The Miller's Dance, or the *farruca* performed by Massine, is the link between flamenco and classical ballet. Below is an analysis of the Miller's Dance performed by Patrick Dupond of the Paris Opera Ballet. It is 2 minutes and 15 seconds in length. The Spanish terminology of the dance steps is

DOI: 10.4324/9781003366928-12

included. The Spanish steps are compared to similar ballet steps, and point out the steps that are unique to ballet if any.

The Miller's Dance

The dancer begins kneeling on his left knee, *arrodillarse*, and claps his hands with muffled sounds, *palmas sordas*. The dancer rises, *rastreado*, facing a diagonal downstage right, *en diagonal anterior derecho*. He takes one step, *semipunta*, or on half-pointe, *paseo de farruca*, on his left leg with the right leg bent in *attitude* pose, *actitud*, and the left arm is front in fourth position palms down. The movement is repeated with the other leg, followed by running steps, *carrerilla*, then fast double stamps, *golpes*, right and left twice, and hands flat on pelvis. With parallel feet on *semipunta*, arms in fourth position with right arm front, the dancer performs a half turn to the left, *media vuelta semipunta*, changes arms to fourth position with left arm front to downstage left, *en diagonal anterior izquierdo*. The *actitud* in this dance is similar to the attitude in ballet, though in ballet the dancer holds the leg higher. The *media vuelta semipunta* is closely akin to *détourné* in ballet.

En diagonal, the dancer takes a step left with parallel feet *semipunta* pose, *remate*, and the left arm opens with the right front in fourth position, then changes back to the left arm. He stamps, *golpe*, with the right foot front and the left foot back, *semipunta*, and snaps fingers, *pitos*. This is followed by the right foot *golpe, saltado*, on right foot, *cabriola*, half scissor kick, *artasi-otsiko*, with the right leg, and arms in fourth position, palms down, using the opposite arm with the working leg. This is repeated another time left. The left foot *golpe* with right foot *semipunta* is repeated two times, then four times rapidly, with the arms in first position, palms down, and a pressing up and down movement with the hands. The dancer steps on the right foot with the left leg to the side, *paso lado*, and the left arm is straight to the side over the leg with the palm down, and the right arm bent with the palm to the chest. There is a step jump, *saltado*, on the left foot to face upstage, *atras*, and arms are closed with palms facing the chest. A circular movement with the right leg is performed during the jump while facing back, *campanela saltado*. The *saltado* is like the *sauté* in ballet and the *artasi-otsiko* is similar to the ballet *ballotte*. The *cabriola* resembles the *cabriole* in ballet; however, in ballet the knees are usually straight. The *campanela saltado* is similar to a double *rond de jambe en l'air sauté*.

The dancer brings both legs together, and a *salto* with a *media vuelta* is executed with hands flat on the pelvis. This is similar to half of a *tour en l'air* in ballet. The *passo lado* right preparation is made for a pirouette with the arms in fourth position, right arm front. The action is turning back, *vuelta de pirueta hacia atras*. The turn is outside right with the right foot touching below the front of the knee. It is identical to the *pirouette endehors* in classical ballet. In the middle of the turn, the left foot replaces the right on the back of the knee,

Analysis of the Miller's Dance and The Three-cornered Hat Story 65

and the right leg becomes the working leg. The turning action is front, *vuelta de pirueta hacia adelante* which is similar to a *pirouette endedans*. The arms are placed in a low first position for both turns. The dancer falls on the left knee, *caída,* from the *vuelta,* and both hands are placed on the left hip. The arms open from right to left with sweeping movements.

Slowly the dancer rises, *rastreado,* to *actitud,* arms fifth position with wrists bent not rounded. The dancer performs a slow turn, *vuelta,* like the ballet *soutenu* and finishes with the left leg to the side, *lado.* There is a *pas de buret natural* to the right side, *de lado derecho,* with the left leg always crossing three times front, and the left arm straight over the left leg, right arm bent to the chest. This is *pas de bourrée* in ballet. The step finishes with a small *salto* to fourth position facing diagonal left, *en diagonal anterior izquierdo,* and the arms are up with the wrists turned to the right. The dancer steps back with the left foot. The *punta* is front with right foot, shifting weight, *punta* back with left foot, and arms are up snapping fingers, *pitos.* Then the dancer lifts the bent left leg, pivots on the right to the other corner, and hits the left foot with the left hand. This is repeated another two times.

The dancer takes three steps *en diagonal anterior derecho* and executes the *esplante saltado cruzado* into a *paseo caída* facing *en diagonal posterior derecho,* arms in second position. The *esplante saltado cruzado* is similar to the ballet *pas de basque* and with both knees bent resembles a ballet *pas de chat.* The *paseo caído* is repeated another four times *en diagonal posterior derecha.* The arm that corresponds to the front leg is lifted then lowered behind the back with each fall. Fast single *golpes* are performed with arms in first position, and hands perform an over, under, circular movement. The dancer jumps, *salto,* in fourth, left leg stretched straight back, facing *de lado izquierdo,* or stage left. The left arm is up, and the right arm is open to the side. The legs are brought together, and a *media vuelta* is made with a hip swivel, arms open in second, to diagonal on *semipunta.*

The dancer makes three double *golpes,* beginning with the left foot and alternating feet. The hands are flat on the pelvis. There is a step back with the right foot, low arms behind the back, *quinta baja detrás.* The right foot is then brought forward with five *golpes* and the left foot in *semipunta.* The hands perform muffled claps, *palmas sordas.* The right foot is taken back in *semipunta* and brought forward to repeat the *golpes* and *semipunta.* When the right foot is back, the arms are in *quinta baja detrás.* The second time the *golpe* step is repeated, hand claps are *palmas sordas* followed by *palmas secas* or dry claps which are clear and sharp sounding. There are two single claps, one double, and one single. The left leg comes up to an *actitud,* arms in high fifth position, wrists bent. The leg comes down to step preparation with right leg *lado* and *vuelta de pirueta hacia atras,* arms up in fifth position on the turn, to *caída* on the left knee, with the arms in *quinta baja detrás,* fifth low back.

Slowly the dancer rises and steps on the left leg bringing both legs together in fifth position or *quinta semipunta* pose facing back *en diagonal posterior derecho.* Arms are up and wrists crossed. This position is balletic, but it also belongs to Spanish dancing. The dancer begins slowly turning right in place, *en sitio,* with *golpes* and *semipunta.* The step is called *vuelta en cuarto tiempo* and resembles a *pas de bourrée en tournant* in ballet. There is one slow full turn in four steps, wrists are crossed, palms and fingers open, and the hands flutter. This is followed by another two *golpe* with *semipunta* to face front, then one *golpe* with *semipunta* to face back, repeat to front, repeat back, front, and back. The right arm opens forward guiding the turns, and the left arm replaces it on the turn. The dancer performs two *golpe* with *semipunta* facing *atras.* The arms are in a closed, locked position behind the back and they sway right, left, right with the two *golpes.*

With the left leg, the dancer steps side and slowly drags the right leg to the back of the left in a *balanceado cruzado,* which is similar to the *balance* in ballet, then executes a *glisada* to the right and another *balanceado cruzado* to the right. The arm that is forward corresponds to the leg that is placed back. The *glisada* is similar to the *glissade* in ballet. The step is repeated to the left, but the second *balanceado* is substituted with *echado* into a *matalarana* right. The *echado* is a ballet *jeté,* and the *matalarana* is a *pas de chat* in ballet. This is repeated again from the *balanceada cruzado* left and *echado* with *matalarana* two more times but faster as the music builds speed and facing forward. The left arm is in fourth position on the first *matalarana* and in fifth on the third and fourth. The four *balanceado* combinations have been made in a semi-circle, and the dancer finishes in the center facing the audience, *adelente.* The dancer performs *golpe* with *semipunta* three times fast with the right leg front to *en diagonal anterior izquierdo.* The front right leg is taken to the back, with one *golpe* and *semipunta.* The step is repeated another three times. The arms are straight to high fifth position on the first three *golpes,* then they sweep back quickly in *quinta baja detrás* on the single *golpe* and *semipunta* back.

The dancer turns on the back foot to face *en diagonal posterior derecho* and takes small running steps, *carrerillas,* to the right corner. The right arm is up and the left arm is side. The *carrerilla* is like the ballet *pas couru.* Then, there is a *salto* into a preparation with the right leg *lado,* right arm in preparation fourth position, and the dancer takes a full run to *en diagonal anterior derecho,* ending with a *voltereta,* or an acrobatic slide on the floor to a finish, *remate,* in a standing fifth position with arms in first position, palms together, one facing up and the other down.

Notes

1 George Balanchine and Francis Mason, *101 Stories of the Great Ballets.* (New York: Dolphin Book Doubleday & Company Inc., 1975), 495–7.
2 Ibid., 496.

Figure 13.1 The flamenco dancer Juana Cala photographed during a performance. Her expression demonstrates the essence of duende, a heightened emotional state necessary in flamenco dance.

Source: Photo by Christopher Scalzi.

13 *Duende*

The interior "raging flame" that flares up during the flamenco dancer's performance is the embodiment of *duende*, the expression and the soul of flamenco dance. Flamenco begins internally and the dancer expresses their own story with or without an audience. Classical ballet is more external because it follows the narrative dictated by a written story, and the dancer performs exclusively for the audience. Expression in flamenco is critical to an authentic interpretation in the dance performance and different from classical ballet. An intrinsic part of flamenco dance is drama, and the dancer communicates this through different facial expressions, for example, contractions of the eyebrows or *fruncimientos de entrecejos*. Also, the deepest emotions of the dancers are projected through body gestures.

The word *expression* is interchangeable with dance and drama, just as the Indian equivalent *natya*. The *Natya Shastra* of Indian dance, the origin of flamenco, has an entire study on expression called the *satvik abhinaya*. Reginald Massey described it in his book on kathak dance:

> **Satvik abhinaya** represents physical manifestations of various mental and emotional states.... Now in real life these manifestations are produced involuntarily, but the dancer, using *satvik abhinaya*, has to induce them voluntarily. This means a supreme control of the mind, so that the dancer can not only turn the tap on, so to speak, but is also able to turn it off at will.[1]

Kathak and bharatanatyam, the foundation of kathak, have similarities and differences in expression or *natya*. Kathak has a very delicate and understated emotional *natya*, whereas bharatanatyam is strong and precise. However, both can claim to be interpretations of *duende*. These subtle expressions of inner emotions break out into striking reactionary gestures. This is the definition of *duende* which is the inspiration of flamenco.[2] Both classical ballet and kathak dancers use mime and movements of the head and hands to bring out emotions or express the idea of a character. The difference is in kathak dance where the whole body is used to illustrate an image. In classical ballet, the dance steps accompany the mime and gestures.[3]

DOI: 10.4324/9781003366928-13

The Spanish word *compás* means rhythm or time. According to the flamenco teacher Irene Rimer, a dancer must feel the *compás* rather than counting the beats because flamenco is an "art-form mastered by intuition." Flamenco is personal for every dancer, singer, and musician so that each performer interprets the art form in a different way. Performers are free to improvise according to what they feel at that moment, but at the same time, they must conform to the frame of the dance.

At the Vivo Carlota Santana Flamenco School in New York, I witnessed the spirit of *duende* from the great master teacher Juana Cala. At one point during a class, the teacher/choreographer assumed the role of artist/dancer. The expression of pain appeared to consume her meditative face, and the deep suffering of the flamenco dancer emerged—the true eruption of inner feelings. Sentiment burst forth not as the imitation of a character or role but as a profound experience of ecstasy while she executed her choreography. The internal fire and passion that I witnessed in flamenco is usually missing in a classical ballet performance.

According to the ancient Greeks, all forms of art, including dance, contain the *Apollonian* and *Dionysian* phenomena. The *Apollonian* elements in art forms are considered solemn, ordered, and perfect, whereas *Dionysian* attributes are irrational, passionate, and sensual. However, while *Apollonian* and *Dionysian* are always present they are rarely equal in an artwork, but when they are, the balance creates a masterpiece.[4] This balance is present in Massine's *Farruca*. His technique was cultivated by the study of flamenco and perfected by years of classical ballet training, but there is the integration of passion and sensuality which belongs to *duende*. The *Dionysian* trance of flamenco dancers is described as

> a fervor, an unchaining of the senses, a paroxysm uniting a singer in Moscow and a dancer in Seville, Ankara musicians and Jerez *buleaeros* in the same raging flame.[5]

The 18th-century German writer and statesman, Goethe, defined *duende* as "a mysterious power that everyone feels and no philosopher can explain."[6] It can be paragoned to "A dance on a tightrope stretched to breaking point"[7] and the moment that the flamenco dancer can no longer restrain the implosion of emotion. This is achieved through the everyday risk of living and cannot be taught, nor can it repeat itself. It is best generalized as "outrageous expressivity."[8] The Spanish poet, playwright, and theater director Federico García Lorca wrote this about *duende* "The duende, is not in the throat, but from within, from the very soles of the feet."[9]

The ballerina, Tamara Karsavina, worried that without the experience of Spanish culture she would not be able to interpret the role of the miller's wife in *The Three-cornered Hat*. Diaghilev asked Massine's flamenco teacher, Félix Fernández García, to perform for Karsavina in the ballroom of the

Savoy Hotel in London where the Ballets Russes members were residing. She recounted what she witnessed at his performance:

> I could feel the impetuous, half-savage instincts within him.... The rhythm of his steps, now staccato, now a whisper, and then again seeming to fill the large room with thunder, made this unseen performance all the more dramatic. We listened to the dancing enthralled.[10]

Duende is the lifeblood of flamenco and can be felt in the *zapateado* steps that connect the earth to the soul of the dancer.

When *The Three-cornered Hat* opened in London, the English poet T.S. Eliot wrote of Massine's performance "Massine ... seems to me the greatest actor whom we have in London."[11] Eliot said, "the abstract gesture of Massine, which *symbolizes* emotion, is enormous."[12] He felt that "emotion in art must be transmitted through physical images analogous to the emotion."[13] These physical images come from life experience, which is the principle of *duende* in flamenco. Eliot went on to write, "the art of every actor is in relation to his own age, and would perhaps be unintelligible to any other."[14] Massine experienced the horrors of war at an early age and perhaps this helped him to feel "the cry of man mortally wounded by destiny"[15] that the Romani proclaim in flamenco. Massine described his performance of the *farruca*:

> I felt instinctively that something more than perfect technique was needed here, but it was not until I had worked myself up in a frenzy that I was able to transcend my usual limitations ... I felt an almost electrical interaction between myself and the spectators.... For one moment it seemed as if some other person within me was performing the dance.[16]

As mentioned before, the *farruca* is "pure dancing" and not a narrative about a life struggle expressed in steps and movements. However, the dancer's level of technical virtuosity is what tells us a story of passion, hard work, and sacrifice reflecting their daily life for years. *Duende,* or the eruption of expressivity, is channeled through the steps and movements of "pure dancing," and Massine's performance in *The Three-cornered Hat* epitomizes this.

Notes

1. Reginald Massey, *India's Kathak Dance, Past, Present, and Future* (New Delhi, India: Abhinav Publications, 1999), 12.
2. Ibid., 38.
3. Ibid., 39.
4. Carol Lee, *Ballet in the Western Culture, A History of Its Origins and Evolution* (Needham Heights, MA: Allyn and Bacon, 1999), 2.
5. Bernard Leblon, *Gypsies and Flamenco* (Hatfield, Hertfordshire: University of Hertfordshire Press, 1994), 8.

6 Ibid., 10.
7 Ibid., 10.
8 Ibid., 8.
9 Ibid., 10.
10 Vicente García-Márquez, *Massine: A Biography* (New York: Knopf, 1995), 132–3.
11 Ibid., 140.
12 Ibid., 140.
13 Ibid., 140.
14 Ibid., 140.
15 Leblon, 55.
16 García-Márquez, 136.

14 In the Footsteps of Massine

The Russian choreographer Leonide Massine should not be accused of cultural appropriation when he choreographed the ballet *The Three-cornered Hat*. Around the same period in Massachusetts, Ted Shawn and Ruth St. Denis were criticized for their exploitation of indigenous dance forms at Jacob's Pillow. There was no assimilation or replication of the dance movements belonging to these cultures in their choreography. The mutual exchange and transculturation was not present but only the traditional costumes. But Shawn and St. Denis succeeded in bringing an awareness of native and oriental dance forms. Massine immersed himself in the Spanish culture and studied flamenco. He absorbed the spirit of the dance, people, and the country with notable appreciation according to his memoir. The choreographer used steps in flamenco and Spanish dance that have similar steps in classical ballet, so he did not create a cultural hybrid.

Early in the creative process, Massine wanted flamenco dancers to perform his ballet rather than dancers from the Ballets Russes. But flamenco dancers and musicians improvise their art. Also, their movements recount their own personal story and not that of the ballet. This presented an enormous problem for the choreographer and composer, so ultimately classical ballet dancers performed *The Three-cornered Hat*. But the music, costumes, and set designs were made by two great Spanish artists, Manuel de Falla and Pablo Picasso, and the story was borrowed from the Spanish theater. Massine's choreography of *The Three-cornered Hat* does not fit the definition of cultural appropriation suggested in the Denis Shawn's works.

A breakdown of the *farruca* and the argument for the authenticity of each step as flamenco or classical ballet are established in the aforementioned analysis. How much of one dance form or the other Massine used in his choreography is debated. The question of how one dance form, flamenco, is able to complement another form, classical ballet, was examined. Both dance forms definitely complemented and influenced each other from the moment of their historical union in 1917 with Diaghilev's Ballets Russes. While flamenco and classical ballet evolved separately through diverse encounters over time, a third dance form was not born from their union.

74 In the Footsteps of Massine

The historical information found in the pages of this book focused on timelines, geography, social and political influences, and similarities and differences between flamenco and classical ballet. The findings constructed the groundwork for this book. The journey and evolution of flamenco from India to Spain fascinated me beyond what I discovered. The discredited theory that the Romani had traveled through Egypt before landing on the European continent was nevertheless an intriguing idea that I could not abandon. Why did the Romani who brought flamenco to the shores of Spain insist they came from Egypt? This question remains unanswered.

Classical ballet yielded extensive research material from writings, paintings, and sculptures, whereas more information emerged on flamenco after the Romani arrived in Spain. Aside from the historical contribution, this study challenges the idea of the language of dance movement tracing the trail of small populations over time. Comparisons and contrasts are made between character dance, the bolero school, flamenco, classical ballet, and Spanish folk dance. In order to decipher Massine's choreography, it was necessary to distinguish each form separately.

The bolero school shares a huge vocabulary of steps and movements from Italian and French classical ballet, but they added their own style from Spanish folk dancing. Both flamenco and the bolero school have borrowed steps from each other. The Spanish regional dances were also assimilated into flamenco and imitated in character dance, so the overlap can create confusion. When an individual dance is analyzed like the *farruca*, the mix of other dance forms must be considered. Classes at the University of Oklahoma were the beginning of my analysis on the compatibility of classical ballet with flamenco. One example was the choreography of a group of flamenco *zapateado* steps followed by three *chainé* turns into a *saltado pose*. The *chaînés* belong to classical ballet, but the Spanish version, *vuelta de pasos*, belonged to the *escuela bolera* with its foundation in classical ballet.

My thoughts on a fusion of flamenco and classical ballet changed as I furthered my research over the course of time. The word "fusion" comes to mind as a permanent, inseparable blend, but each dance form, flamenco and classical ballet, exists by itself. Thus, the word "union" better describes the way these two dance forms work together. Flamenco and classical ballet retain their individual form but are complemented by their partnership. I examined the combination of other dance forms when they are used together, and the result of this observation determined that two dance forms are never equally represented in choreography. The choreographer is the creator and can add or subtract steps and movements in a dance or piece, according to his or her creative impulse, without set rules.

Before the *farruca* or Miller's dance in the *Tricorne* even begins, the difference between flamenco and classical ballet is striking. The flamenco *cuadro*, a group of dancers and musicians, performed on small stages or *tablao* in nightclubs and later moved to theaters. Classical Ballet performed on large stages for at least 100 years when the Ballets Russes arrived in Spain. Massine was able to use more space in his choreography, so at first glance, the *farruca* resembles a ballet with its spatial quality. However, the classical ballet steps are also *escuela bolero* steps combined with flamenco, in the choreography of the Miller's dance.

The dispersion of the steps diverts the audience from the traditional dance, and the viewer sees a Spanish style ballet painted with broad brushstrokes. Here at work we see the true genius of Leonide Massine. For example, the *caída*, or fall which belongs to the *farruca* dance, is repeated five times on a diagonal. The step covers the distance from one end of the stage to the other. The use of space gives the *caída* a ballet quality to a flamenco step.

The technique of classical ballet applied to different dance forms will enhance the performance in a proscenium setting, and this can be seen in the Miller's Dance. The higher and stronger execution of all jumps in the *farruca* is noteworthy in the performance of Paris Opera's Patrick Dupond in *Tricorne*, along with his precision in all turns. This represents the *Apollonian* factor of solemn control and perfection that is necessary to classical Ballet. The *Dionysian* factor is the inner expression of passion and sensuality which is essential to Spanish dancing. The union of both the *Apollonian* and *Dionysian* is the partnership or marriage of flamenco and classical ballet exhibited in the Miller's Dance in *The Three-cornered Hat*. The steps of both dance forms did not melt together, but the style and technique of classical ballet united with the flamenco steps in the Miller's Dance.

What can flamenco and classical ballet share with each other? In flamenco, there is an emphasis on the upper part of the body: hands, arms, and the back. The arched back of the flamenco dancer is similar to the posture of the swan in *Swan Lake*. Arms create more shapes in flamenco, and the study of Spanish hand movements would benefit classical ballet dancers. Musicality is improved with the study of flamenco *zapateado* and *palmas* or hand clapping. The contact with the floor is another important study that can benefit classical ballet.

The energetic footwork pushing down into the floor creates a trajectory that ignites the soul and spirit in movement. This contact with the earth erupts and explodes in the dancer revealing the unexplainable emotion of *duende*. It is this powerful channeling of sufferance that tests our lives or the sheer joy of reaching an incredible goal. This is the passion of dance. More *duende* is needed in classical ballet rather than the total dedication to technical perfection and virtuosity.

There is no doubt that the study of classical ballet can help the flamenco dancer have a more superb and elegant technique. Many flamenco schools have introduced classical ballet to their curriculum because of Diaghilev's influence. His Ballets Russes Company stimulated artistic curiosity all over Spain, and one could argue that the presence of the Ballets Russes in Spain helped to elevate flamenco from the *café de cante* to the theatrical stage.

The work of Diaghilev and Massine continues 100 years later with the National Ballet of Spain, a dance company that combines both flamenco and classical ballet with great success around the world today. My hope is that this book will inspire and encourage choreographers to find a mutual relationship with other dance forms and ballet as Leonide Massine did with *The Three-cornered Hat*. The historical meeting of the Ballets Russes and flamenco in Spain can ultimately be summarized in these words:

Like all important cultural phenomena it was born of encounter.[1]

The passion of flamenco married the elegance of classical ballet when they met at the Ballets Russes.

Note

1 Bernard Leblon, *Gypsies and Flamenco* (Hatfield, Hertfordshire: University of Hertfordshire Press, 1994), 78.

Bibliography

Balanchine, George, and Francis Mason. *101 Stories of the Great Ballets*. New York: Dolphin Book Doubleday & Company, Inc, 1975.
Buonaventura, Wendy. *Serpent of the Nile: Women and Dance in the Arab World*. Northampton, MA: Interlink Books, 2010.
Caroso, Fabritio. *Nobilità di Dame, 1600*. Translated and edited by Julia Sutton. New York: Dover Publications, Inc., 1995.
Charnon-Deutsch, Lou. *The Spanish Gypsy, The History of a European Obsession*. University Park: The Pennsylvania State University Press, 2004.
Garafola, Lynn. *Diaghilev's Ballets Russes*. New York and Oxford: Oxford University Press, 1989.
Garafola, Lynn, and Nancy Van Norman Baer. *The Ballets Russes and Its World*. New Haven, CT: Yale University Press, 1999.
García-Márquez, Vicente. *Massine: A Biography*. New York: Knopf, 1995.
Goldberg, K. Meira, Ninotchka Devorah Bennahum, and Michelle Heffner Hayes. *Flamenco on the Global Stage, Historical, Critical, and Theoretical Perspectives*. Jefferson, NC: McFarland & Company, Inc., 2015.
Grut, Marina. *The Bolero School*. England: Dance Books, 2002.
Leblon, Bernard. *Gypsies and Flamenco*. Hatfield: University of Hertfordshire Press, 1994.
Lee, Carol. *Ballet in Western Culture, A History of Its Origins and Evolution*. Needham Heights, MA Allyn and Bacon, 1999.
Lexová, Irene. *Ancient Egyptian Dances*. Mineola, New York: Dover Publications, Inc, 2000.
Massey, Reginald. *India's Kathak Dance, Past, Present, Future*. New Delhi, India: Abhinav Publications, 1999.
Massine, Leonide. *My Life in Ballet*. London: MacMillan, 1968.
Pagels, Jurgen. *Character Dance*. Bloomington: Indiana University Press, 1984.
Percival, John. *The World of Diaghilev*. Great Britain: Studio Vista/Dutton Pictureback, 1971.
Philips, Miriam. "Hopeful Futures and Nostalgic Past." In Flamenco on the Global Stage, Historical, Critical, and Theoretical Perspectives, edited by K. Meira Goldberg, Ninotchka Devorah Bennahum, and Michelle Heffner Hayes, 47. Jefferson, NC: McFarland & Company, 2015.
Steingress, Gerhard. "Antecedents of Carmen in the History of Spanish Dance." In *Flamenco on the Global Stage, Historical, Critical, and Theoretical Perspectives*,

edited by K. Meira Goldberg, Ninotchka Devorah Bennahum, and Michelle Heffner Hayes, 121. Jefferson, NC: McFarland & Company, 2015.

Vittucci, Matteo Marcellus. *The Language of Spanish Dance, A Dictionary and Reference Manual*. 2nd ed. Princeton, NJ: Princeton Book Company, 2003.

Films

Massine, Leonide. *Spanish Dancers*. MGZIDF 4750 MGZHB 2-1000 #268. New York: New York Public Library for the Performing Arts, 1917.

Paris Opera Ballet: Picasso and Dance, Tricorne. New Hope, PA: Kultur Video, 2005.

Staats, Leo, Leonide Massine, and Nikolai Legat. MGZIC 9-2788. New York: New York Public Library for the Performing Arts, 1929–1930.

Index

Note: Page references in *italics* refer to the figures.

101 Stories of the Great Ballets (Balanchine and Mason) 63

Académie Royale de Danse 28
Académie Royale de Musique 28
aficionado 20
Alarcón, Pedro Antonio de 47
alegrías 53
Alexander the Great 6, 23
Alfonso XIII, King of Spain 46
alpargatas 57
Ancient Egyptian Dances (Lexová) 10
Angiolini, Gasparo 33
Anna, Czarina 33
anti-Romani law 19
Apollo (Stravinsky) 39, 41
Apollo et Daphne (Didelot) 34
Apollonian factor 70, 75
Arabic dance 4, 14–16
Aryans 3, 5
Aurora's Wedding 42

Baer, Nancy Van Norman 41
bail del candil 20
baile teatral (dance-drama) 12
Bakst, Leon 39
Balanchine, George 1, 41, 63
ballet d'action 28, 29
Ballet de Cour 26
Ballet in Western Culture, A History of Origins and Evolution (Lee) 23
Ballets Russes 1, 20, *38*, 39–42; artistic strength of 40; nomadic life of 42; origins of 32–36; season in London 41

The Ballets Russes and its World (Garafola and Baer) 41
Banjara 2
barre 52
Beauchamp, Pierre 27–28
Beaujoyeulx, Balthasar de 26
Benois, Alexander 39
Berlin Museum 12
bharata 6
bharatanatyam 1, 69
Bharata Natya Shastra 6
Blasis, Carlo 57
Bolchakov, Anatoli Petrovich 46
bolero school 54–55, 74
The Bolero School (Grut) 54
boles 8
Book of Kings 2
botillerias 20
Bournonville, A. 54–55
Bournonville style 54
Brahmin 5
Buddhism 6
bulerias 15, 53
Buonaventura, Wendy 2
Byzantine influence 25
Byzantine music 25

Cachucha (Elssler) *22*, 30
Cachucha costume *22*
Cadiz (Gadez) 14, 19
caída 58
Cala, Juana *18*, *68*, 70
cambre 16
Cambyses II of Persia 3
canto jondo 4, 25
Carmona, Angel Pericet 56

Index

Caroso, Fabritio 26
Casanova, G. 57
castes 5
Cecchetti, Enrico 35, 40
chakkar (pirouette) 7, 10–11
character dance 51–56; 1909 to 1929 53;
    comparison and contrast with
    flamenco dance 51; European
    countries 51; examples of 51;
    musical counts 53; rules of
    classical ballet 52
Charles Davillier, Jean 3, 20
Charles III 19, 28
Charnon-Deutsch, Lou 3
Châtelet Theater, Paris 40
chelas (students) 6
Chopiniana 40
Christian burials 24
ciguena (stork) pose 10
Cinderella 35
clappers 11
classical ballet 1, 16, 23–30; flamenco
    dance and 23–30; folk dancing
    in Europe 24; origins 23; in
    Spain 27
classical Indian dance 5
The Code of Terpsichore (Blasis) 57
commedia dell'arte 28, 29, 33
compás 4, 70
contratiempo 59
Coppélia (Saint-Léon) 30, 51
coreodramma 29
Cornell University 12
Corregidor 63
costumed singers and dancers 24–25
Court dancing 24
cuadro flamenco 15
Czingany 3

dance 5–6; *desi* 6; *natya* 6; *nritta* 6;
    nritya 6; parts 6; terminology 6;
    see also specific dance
Danilova, Alexandra 1
danse d'école 28, 33
Dauberval, Jean 29
desi dance 6
Diaghilev, Serge 1, 30, 32, 36, 39–42,
    45–48, 53, 70, 73, 75–76
Diaghilev's World (Percival) 39
Didelot, Charles-Louis 34
Dionysian factor 70, 75
Don Quixote 1, 46, 51, 55
Doré, Gustav 20

Doubrovska, Felia 1
drama 5
dramatic dance 12
duende 53, 69–71
Dupond, Patrick 63

Egyptian dance 10–13; musical
    instruments 10; public outdoor
    dancing 11
An Egyptian Night (Fokine) 40
El amor brujo (Falla) 47
El Corregidor y la molinera 47
Eliot, T.S. 71
Elssler, Fanny 22, 30
escuelo bolero (Spanish folk dance) 12,
    16, 30, 53

Falla, Manuel de 4, 46, 47, 63, 73
fandango 57–58
farruca 58–60, 71, 73, 74
felah mengu (peasant flight) 14
Ferdinand of Aragon 25
Ferdinand V 19
Fernández, Francesco León 28
Fernández García, Félix 45, 47–48, 70
The Firebird 39
flamenco dance 1–4; *canto jondo* 4;
    classical ballet and 23–30;
    contrasts and similarities to
    other dance forms 51–56;
    fandango 57–58; *farruca* 58–60;
    history of 1–2; kathak dance 1;
    in Spain 19–21, 45–49
Flamenco International Magazine 54
Flamenco on the Global Stage
    (Goldberg, Bennahum, and
    Hayes) 3, 27
Fokine, Michel 40, 46
folk dancing in Europe 24
forbidden dance 14
Franconetti, Silvio 20
free-standing scenery 26
French Court of King Louis XIV 23
French Revolution 29

Gadez dancers 14
Garafola, Lynn 36, 41
García-Márquez, Vicente 45
Gautier, Theophile 20
gharana 7
ghawazee 12–13
ghaziya 12
ghungurus 7

Giselle 30, 34
gitanos 3, 13, 28
Godunov, Boris 40
Gorsky, Alexander 45
Granada 25
Greek civilization 23
Greek cultural tradition of dance 23
Greek dramas 23
Greek plays 23
Gregorian chant 25
Grisi, Carlotta 30
Grut, Marina 54
guitar 10
guru vandanan in Indian dance 15
Gypsies and Flamenco: The Emergence of the Art of Flamenco in Andalusia (Leblon) 4

Harappa 5
hastas in kathak 7
Hindu 2
Hinduism 6
Houara 4
Houara performance 15
Houara tribe 15
humanism 25

Imperio, Pastora 47
India: dance in 5; dance profession in 7; drama in 5; Marwar Nautch dancer of 15
Indian classical music 4
Indian Ragas 4
India's Kathak Dance, Past, Present, Future (Massey) 5
Industrial Revolution 29
Isabella I 19
Isabella of Castile 25
Italian Renaissance 25
Ivanov, Lev 36

jaleo 15
joglars 24
jota 10

Karsavina, Tamara 48–49, *62*, 70
kathak dance 1–2, 69; *hastas* in 7; history of 5; *mudras* in 7; origins of 5–8; schooling of 5; school of 7; in Vedic period 5
Khandala, India 8
King Louis XIII 26
King Louis XIV 27

Koran 15
Krishna (Hindu god) 5
Krishna Lila 8
Kschessinka, Mathilda 36

La Bayadère (Petipa) 34, 35
La Camargo 28
La Fille Mal Gardee (Dauberval) 29
La Forza dell'amore e dell'odio 33
Lafuente, Rafael 3
The Language of Spanish Dance, A Dictionary and Reference Manual (Vittucci) 7
Las Meninas (Velázquez) 47
La Sylphide (Taglioni) 29
Law of Philip IV 27
Le Ballet Comique de la Reine (the Dramatic Ballet of the Queen) 26
Leblon, Bernard 3–4
Le Déliverance De Renaud (The Liberation of Renaud) 26–27
Lee, Carol 23
The Legend of Joseph (Fokine) 41, 46
Legnani, Pierina 35
Le Pavillon d'Armide (Fokine) 40
Les Noces (Nijinska) 41
Le Spectre de la Rose 39
Les Sylphides 39, 40; *see also Chopiniana*
The Letters on Dancing and Ballets (Noverre) 29
Lexová, Irene 10
The Little Hump-backed Horse (Saint-Léon) 34
London Alhambra Theater 21
Louis XIV, King of France 27–28, 32
Lully, Jean-Baptiste 27–28

Maazin, Yousef 12–13
margi 6
Martínez Síerras group 47
Marwar Nautch dancer of India 15
Mason, Francis 63
Massey, Reginald 5, 8, 69
Massine, Leonide 8, 20–21, 33, 41, 45–49, *62*, 73–76
Massine, Tatiana 60
Massine: A Biography (García-Márquez) 45
Medici, Catherine de 26
Medici, Lorenzo di 26
Menaka 8

Index

Menaka Lasyam 8
meneo 16
Middle Eastern dance 1–2
Miller's Dance 63, 64–66
minstrels 24
Mohenjo Daro 5
Molière 27–28
Montoya, Ramon 58
Moors 19, 23–24
Morisco Andaluza 16
Moriscos 19
Morocco 15
Moscow Imperial Theater 45–46
mudras in kathak 7
munecas 16
musical instruments 10
Muslim religion 15
My Life in Ballet (Massine) 48

nataka 5–6
natya 6
Natya Shastra 4, 14, 69; *see also* Bharata Natya Shastra
Navarro, Juan de Esquivel 27
New York Public Library for the Performing Arts 60
Nijinska, Bronislava 41
Nijinsky, V. 40–41
Nobilità di Dame (Caroso) 26
Noverre, Jean Georges 28
nritta 6, 7
nritta hastas 7
nritya 6
Nutcracker 1, 51

off-beat rhythms 8
ondulado 16
Oriental music 4

Pagels, Jurgen 51
Palillos 12
Paquita 1
Parade 41–42
Paris Opera 30, 34, 55, 63, 75
paseo de farruca 59
paseo de zambra 15
paso de caída 58
Pavane (Fauré) 47
Pavlova, Anna 8
pavonear 7
peacock gait *(chaals)* 7
pellizcos 7
pelvis *(trika)* 14

Percival, John 39
Pericet system 56
Perrot, Jules 34
Persia 2–3
Peter the Great 32–33
Petipa, Marius 34–36, 40–42, 55
Petrouchka (Fokine) 39, 46
Petrovich, Anatoli 47
Philips, Miriam 3
Phrygian scale/mode 12
Picasso, Pablo 42, 48, 63, 73
pirouette endedan 10
Polovtsian Dances 53
Prince Igor (opera) 40, 53
The Prodigal Son (Prokofiev) 41
professional dancers 12
Protestant Reformation 27
Psamtik III of Egypt 3

quebrada 16
quinta 11

remachos 59
Renaissance court ballets 24
reverence 15
reverencia 15
rhythms, off-beat 8
Richelieu, Cardinal 27
The Rite of Spring (Nijinsky) 41
Romani 1–4, 15; in Hungary 3; in India 1–2; nomadic life of 16; in Russia 3; in Spain 3, 25
Royal Courts of India 6
rumba gitana 20, 52

sacred dance 6
Saint-Léon, Arthur 30, 34
Sanskrit 2
sarabande 27
satvik abhinaya 69
Scheherazade 47
Seguidilla (Bournonville) 55
Shastras 5–6
Shawn, Ted 73
siguiriyas 12
single dancer 12
Sinti 13
Sleeping Beauty (Petipa) 34, 36
The Sleeping Princess 41
soleares 53
Spain 1–2, 19–21; *baile teatral* (dance-drama) in 12; Romani in 25; styles of Spanish dance in 51

Spanish dance 1
*The Spanish Gypsy, The History
    of a European Obsession*
    (Charnon-Deutsch) 3
Spanish Muslims 25
Stanislavsky, Konstantin 46
St. Denis, Ruth 73
Stravinsky, Igor 36, 41
Swan Lake (Petipa) 34, 46, 51, 75
Swinburne, Henry 19

tablao 51
tableau vivant 12
Taglioni, Marie 29, 34
tal 4
tambourines/castanets 11–12
Tchaikovsky, Peter 36
Thérèse, Marie 33
The Three-cornered Hat 1, 8, 23, 33,
    35–36, 39, 45, 48–49, 54, 60,
    63–66, 70–71, 73
tiempo 11
tiempo de farruca 59
tourism 20
traveling dancers and musicians 12
Travels in Spain (Gautier) 20
*Travels through Spain in the Years 1775
    & 1776* (Swinburne) 19
Treatise on the Art of Dancing
    (Navarro) 27
Tricorne 21, 29

troubadours 24
Tsingane 3
tukra 7, 8
Twiss, Richard 58

upper-class social dances 24

Vaishnavite Cult 5
Vargas, Juana 20
Vargas, Juana, *La Macarrona* 20
Velásquez, D. 47
Vijaya Nritya 8
Vishnu (Hindu god) 5
Vittucci, Matteo Marcellus 7, 53
Vladimirov, Pierrre 1
Voyage in Spain (Charles Davillier) 20
vuelta ciguena 10
vuelta de zambra 15
vuelta quebrada 15
vuelta quebradita 58, 59

The World of Art 40

Yepes, Ana 27

Zalema 15
Zambra Mora (Moorish dance) 12,
    14–15, 19
zapateado 59
Zarabanda 27
zarandilla 14–15

For Product Safety Concerns and Information please contact our EU representative GPSR@taylorandfrancis.com
Taylor & Francis Verlag GmbH, Kaufingerstraße 24, 80331 München, Germany

www.ingramcontent.com/pod-product-compliance
Lightning Source LLC
Chambersburg PA
CBHW051758230426
43670CB00012B/2340